WHY CHRIST?

BY

James Kelly, O.S.B.

Bloomington, IN Milton Keynes, UK

authorHOUSE®

AuthorHouse™
1663 Liberty Drive, Suite 200
Bloomington, IN 47403
www.authorhouse.com
Phone: 1-800-839-8640

AuthorHouse™ UK Ltd.
500 Avebury Boulevard
Central Milton Keynes, MK9 2BE
www.authorhouse.co.uk
Phone: 08001974150

First published by AuthorHouse 8/21/2006

ISBN: 1-4259-4938-X (sc)

Library of Congress Control Number: 2006906259

Printed in the United States of America
Bloomington, Indiana

This book is printed on acid-free paper.

WHY CHRIST?

WHY?

The young man had been asking himself: where am I going? what lies ahead? Yet these were not the focus of his thinking. Nor was the growing realization that he had a poor self image. These were all secondary to a deep conviction that he was really unhappy.

The "young man" represents every man and woman, young or old, who is seeking and searching for security, for happiness. This young man was a baptized Christian, but he had never truly lived his faith. His parents were devout, and he had learned the basics of belief, but he didn't know the way. In this story he meets someone who *does*.

The one who does know the way is an "old man" and wise, a man who radiates the peace and the happiness the young man is seeking. When the old man was a young man he encountered Jesus and followed Him. His happiness reflects his knowing he has a friend, a faithful friend. He assures the young man that he too is sometimes unhappy, from trying circumstances or simple fatigue, but never for long. This is because the Friend he found in his youth is still with him; he's not alone.

The old man shared his experience of Jesus, for him the best way to peace and happiness. It is the way to know what God has planned for each of us, to know what ultimately lies ahead. Meanwhile, we're not alone, unless we want to be. God wants to be with us....

I'm a biblical scholar who lived several years in Jerusalem, studying the texts of the Bible and its background: the languages, the culture, and the history. I also learned from the Land itself, from the people Jesus knew, His own people. They are still there, in their descendants, whether Jewish or Arabic, the same Semitic people. Knowing the land and its culture helps us to understand God's word, the Bible, and His ultimate word, Jesus the Christ. He *is* God's full self revelation.

My models: For the "young man" I remember many young men and women who've come to me over the years, with the same questions in various forms. For the "old man" I have two specific men in my memory, two old men I met in Jerusalem back in the "Sixties!"

The first old man was a Sufi. Sufis can be described by the following narrative of my experience. I had just finished reading a biography of a holy Sufi and wondered if there were any nearby. One morning I mentioned this to the then Director of the French Institute of biblical and archeological studies (the famed Ecole Biblique) in Jerusalem, where I was studying. He told me there were no Sufis in Jerusalem. About an hour later I encountered a Sufi, there in Jerusalem!

It was a warm and pleasant morning of our summer vacation from formal lectures when I started out on my search...not for Sufis but for a Crusader church changed into a mosque. Walking along a narrow winding street in the Muslim quarter of the Old City I met a young Muslim friend who asked me what I was looking for. When I told him he indignantly said: Muslims never do that! At this point an old man came out of the little mosque where I'd stopped. He glowed with the peace and happiness of someone who knows he's loved! Later, I learned that this was "the church!" My friend introduced us. The old man was a Sufi and invited me to their evening prayer.

Having studied Arabic the previous summer in Lebanon and frequently practicing it enabled me to mingle with the people among whom I lived (as my having studied modern Hebrew had done in the Jewish section of the then divided city some time before).

That evening I was welcomed to the little group of about thirty men, of all ages, who sat in a circle and made room for me. When the leader, the sheik, introduced me as a Christian a young man asked who Christ was. The sheik said simply: He was a good man who went about healing the sick.

That room was filled with a peace, the love each man felt and openly expressed for God, Allah.

Islam represents an ancient practice of separating men and women in worship and prayer, so there were only men in this meeting. The peace I had sensed in the old man that morning had obviously been attained at an early age by the younger men. I still hear their sighs as they gently swayed and spoke the name, Allah, prolonging the sound of that word, savoring it, wanting it to linger...

The second old man I'm using as a model was sitting on the floor in a corner of the great Al Aqsa mosque that stands over the now hidden staircase that led up into the Temple area from the lower city in Jesus' time. The staircase remains, and I walked up those steps that Jesus surely climbed!

In those days I had ready access to the vast esplanade that in Jesus' day surrounded the Temple and today holds two of Islam's holiest places. The

Dome of the Rock most probably covers the site of the Temple's Holy of Holies. It now shelters the rock from which Muslims believe Mohammed rode on his steed to heaven. The other great shrine is the enormous Al Aqsa mosque.

One afternoon I was in the near empty mosque, gazing at a famed work of art, when I sensed something negative. I turned to see a fearsome man in the robes of the desert striding towards me, a dagger in his belt, hostility on his face. He was of course not a member of the official caretakers of the shrines. In Arabic he told me to get out, and with as much bravado as I could muster I walked slowly away. I passed an old man sitting in the corner, praying. Having certainly seen everything, he smiled up at me and said, also in Arabic, "welcome."

The gospel of the publican and the Pharisee came to mind! Jesus had promoted humility as a good way to pray: two men, one important, the other humble, came to the Temple (which had stood not far away as Jesus spoke) to pray. The important man thanked God for having made him so much better than others, such as that wretched sinner behind him. The "sinner" just asked God for pardon, and He was the one who went home with peace in his heart.

Now comes the question: if these Muslims could be such good persons, aware of the presence of God in their lives, why search further? If there are, as we know there are, so many beautiful souls among the varied religions of the world. If all men and women, not just Christ's followers, who reflect God's own love will one day share the divine life they now mirror. Why proclaim Jesus Christ? Is there any advantage in knowing Jesus Christ?

Yes! God shows Himself, reveals Himself, in the beauty of creation and most especially in the beauty of men and women who show their love by trying to make others' lives happy. Nevertheless, He has shown Himself perfectly, as He is, in His Son, Jesus Christ. Jesus is the clear and flawless reflection of God the Almighty, the Creator of everything that exists. To know Jesus is to know God. Of no one else can this be said.

To know God already in this life is the happiest state of the human soul. God is the best of all possible friends, the one who knows our hearts better than we ourselves. He loves each of us better than any man or woman can. He forgives us even before we ask. He is the one who understands us. He is the friend who never leaves us, no matter how often we disappoint Him, no matter what we say or do. He is the friend who lived among us, in His Son Jesus the Christ. Jesus whose parting words to His disciples, His friends, as He left them physically said, "I am with you till the end of time."

CONTENTS

THE YOUNG MAN IN
THE HOLY LAND

The young Roman was standing there on the Mount of Olives looking over the city of Jerusalem that was still very beautiful in spite of its much ruined condition from the rebellion of the Jewish people some twenty years before. He had come on a quest, a search for the answer to a question that had occupied the center of his thinking for at least two years now. He'd been asking himself:

"What to do with my life? Why am I alive? My father is rich. My family is loving. I've got everything, but I feel empty. Is this all there is? I'm not happy. I look at so many other people hustling about, worried most of the time, even when they should be happy. I've no direction. Where should I go?"

The young man was Greek by birth, Jewish by heritage. His family had become Christian and had moved to Rome when he was twelve years old. They had taught him the essentials of their faith in Jesus, but he had not paid much attention. It was an older Christian teacher who had advised him to go East, to follow the footsteps of Jesus in the land where He had walked.

Suddenly he became aware of someone sitting there, a few feet from him. As he later told:

" Until he spoke I'd not seen him. I'd just climbed the wide path leading up the Mount of Olives from the Kidron valley that lies between the Mount and Jerusalem. A Christian boy had guided me to the grotto where Jesus had prayed and taught. He had left me there and gone on to the nearby village where a small Christian community still lived.

Jerusalem was responding to the clear morning light shining on its honey hued stones. Across the Kidron I heard sounds of the city now wide awake: metals jingling , donkeys braying, and the best sound of all, human voices. Since Jesus had so often used this grotto he must have often gazed from this same spot on the city He loved.

When I heard the man speak I turned and saw, or so I thought at the time, the oldest man I'd ever seen. He was sitting so quietly, just a few feet away, that he almost blended into the rocky hillside. His attention was fully focused on the city to the west of us, but he must have seen me with the Christian boy and then concluded that I too followed the Way. What he said stunned me and made the day wonderful at its very beginning, for he said, "I was, and am, one of His disciples."

He had known Jesus, and here he was, friendly and obviously eager to talk with me! Without averting his gaze from the city across the way he asked me where I'd come from and why! I told him of my search for meaning in my life as in life itself. His cheerful heart showed itself on his face and in his friendliness. Presuming my Jewish blood he asked:

"Were you taught our Sacred Scriptures in the language of our forebears?"

"Yes, even though my parents became followers of Jesus before I was born, I was brought up in both cultures, Greco-Roman and Hebrew. I can speak the same language Jesus used when He lived here."

At this the old man's face showed his pleasure, and he began to speak the same tongue my grandparents had once spoken in this very land. I said to him:

"You're a happy person!"

He replied:

"That's because I'm always aware of His presence! Yes, fatigue, or the weather, or really negative events can dim this awareness, but not for long. I have to listen, of course, because He speaks to me in various ways. Through other people, through beautiful things, and directly!"

The aged disciple neither asked my name nor gave his, but he did identify himself:

"I'm sure you remember the story of the rich young man Jesus invited to give up his wealth and follow Him? I was that rich young man!"

What could I say? After a minute or two he continued,

"That day was a sad day indeed. I wanted to follow Him but for many reasons I could not give up everything to join the inner core of His disciples. I saw that He loved me, and I loved Him in my own limited way. I knew I had disappointed Him, and that is a terrible experience, to know you have disappointed someone you love and esteem, someone who loves you and expects you to come through for him. I was only a few years older than you are now, but that day is as fresh in my mind as if it happened only yesterday, or earlier today!

2

I found that Jesus was as kind and forgiving as I had thought, for although I did not give up everything I did gradually become a disciple, as did others who did not become part of the inner core of Jesus' followers but became part of His little community. Since I had considerable properties in this area of Judea as well as in Galilee I was able to be with the Brethren from time to time and to help them materially, just as Mary Magdalene and others did.

After His death and rising again I could help Jesus' mother, Mary, and learned much from her memories. Good can indeed come out of evil, for my weakness in being unable to give up everything for Him made me all the more aware of His kindness and patience. I think He too saw this (!) He was, and is, the best friend I ever had.

I was a Galilean and had various business interests there, including fishing boats. I knew Peter slightly but his two friends, James and his brother John well. In fact it was through these closest friends of Jesus that I first heard of Him. Gradually I came to know Peter much more intimately and deepened my friendship with James and John, even as I did my friendship with the Him, the most loyal and faithful of friends.

Many things I can now share with you because I heard and saw them myself, but many other things I heard not only from Mary but from these friends. The essence of what Jesus said and did I do remember, but nobody can recall the exact words and events in every detail. Let me start from the beginning, as do the versions of the gospel you hear in our churches!"

When the young Roman later shared with others what the aged disciple told him about Jesus, of the happiness in knowing beyond doubt that we are loved, He said:

"As he spoke it came to me, as clear as the morning light. I now knew what I'd been looking for, and I knew where I could find it...."

WHEN GOD SHOWED HIMSELF

It was springtime, and the very air was filled with new life, when Mary had a visit from a messenger of God, the angel Gabriel.

This happened during the reign of Caesar Augustus, at Nazareth, a tiny village in the green hills of Galilee. Neither Nazareth nor Mary herself was of any renown at the time. She was an ordinary young woman, barely of marriageable age, promised to Joseph, an older man and carpenter by trade. The Nazarenes would have been surprised to know of Mary's visit, because she was simply one of them.

Mary herself was surprised! There stood the angel Gabriel, before her. The angel said, "don't be afraid. You are loved by God more than any other human being. You will conceive and bear a Son. You will name Him,"Jesus." The Lord God will give Him the throne of David, His father, and He will rule over the house of Jacob forever."

This prophecy, that the Child would rule over Israel, was not so startling in itself. Mary's promised spouse was in fact a descendant of David the King. Mary was more startled, and perplexed, by the announcement of her pregnancy! She prudently asked, "how is this possible, since I am a virgin?"

"The Holy Spirit will come upon you, and the power of the Most High will overshadow you," was the angel's answer. The divine Spirit of life by which the human race, in Adam and Eve, came into being, this same Spirit would place life in Mary's hallowed womb.

Then the angel announced another miraculous event: Mary's elderly cousin, Elizabeth, was seemingly long past the age of childbearing, yet she had conceived six months before, "for nothing is impossible for God!"

Deeply devoted to the study of our ancient Scriptures, Mary saw in this angelic statement an answer to the question posed many centuries before by God Himself. In the guise of an angel, He had asked Abraham, the father of our faith, "is anything impossible for God?"

Do you recall that scene? In the arid land south of Beersheba. Abraham had pitched his tent in a little oasis and was resting from the noonday heat. In the uncertain light he discerned three strangers approaching his camp. Following timeless norms of hospitality, Abraham invited the men to stop and refresh themselves. Unknown to Abraham, he was entertaining God and two of His angels.

God promised him the one thing this rich and powerful man did not have, a son to carry on his name. When Sarah heard that she and Abraham would have a child in their old age, she laughed aloud. Hearing her laugh from behind the tent curtain, God raised His voice and asked why Sarah had laughed. Unthinking, she called out that she had not laughed!

God insisted. She had indeed laughed, but the day would come when she would laugh with joy with a little boy, Isaac. As you know, this name means, "God has laughed."

God left Abraham with a challenging, "is anything impossible for God?"

True daughter of Abraham, father of our faith, Mary responded: "I am the servant of the Lord. Be it done as you have said."

The angel left her, and Mary's first thought was to go and visit her elderly cousin in distant Judea, to help her and to share her happiness and wonder. She let Joseph, her promised husband, know that she was pregnant. At the news he was confused and dismayed. His lovely lady was with child but not by him.

Joseph was a just man, i.e., at peace with God, living according to the Torah, God's revealed guiding word, and he was very much in love with his young bride. His home was Bethlehem, a poor place in Judea; he had come north to Galilee where there was more work for builders and carpenters. I think he had been married, and that this was after the death of his first wife, but my memory is not exact there. Heartbroken, he decided to quietly break their engagement.

The next day he was of a different mind; during the night he'd had a dream. An angel of the Lord had told him Mary was pregnant through the direct intervention of the life giving Spirit of God. Relieved and thankful, Joseph took his beloved into his home as his lawful wife. He arranged for her to join a group of pilgrims about to set out for Jerusalem, to celebrate the Passover in the Holy City.

The little group went down from Nazareth and across the flat fertile plain of Jezreel, then up again through the gentle rounded hills of Samaria. From there they crossed into the land of Judea. Elizabeth and her husband, the priest Zachary, lived in a village near Jerusalem, convenient for his periodic ministry in the Temple.

Zachary was ministering in the Temple, offering incense, when an angel of the Lord appeared and announced to him that he and Elizabeth would have a son. The old priest was incredulous. Mary had prudently asked how a virgin could conceive without sleeping with a man, but she had believed. Zachary did not believe at all that an elderly couple could have a child.

Mary trusted in God's ability to do anything. Zachary did not. For his lack of faith, Zachary was struck dumb. Chastened, he went home to Elizabeth, and she conceived by him.

Mary's Visit to Elizabeth

It was near the end of March, but an unusual cold winter had delayed the blooming of flowers and fruit trees. Now the white and pale pink of the almond blossoms mingled with the pale green of the olive trees. Eager to share her happiness, Mary hurried along the path towards the village just ahead. Even in her haste, she was aware of the beauty around her, bathed as it was in the soft light of spring. It was as if nature was saluting the beauty in the Virgin's womb.

Forgetting the long miles she had walked, Mary almost ran the rest of the way. Her cheerful company was needed in the house ahead. Since the day he had heard and not believed God's word,

Zachary had remained without speech. There were days when Elizabeth's faith faded, yet it never failed. As she heard Mary call to her, this faith revived. She rushed to the door.

Mary often shared the scene with me. She seemed to experience it anew each time she told it. It almost seems as if I too were there, in the village of vineyards, as we called the place.

I can see Mary's face glowing with the wonder of youth and her approaching motherhood. At the sound of Mary's voice Elizabeth experienced the divine presence in her soul. The Spirit touched both her and the baby in her womb. he felt him move, as if dancing! Her spirit soared, and she said:

"What have I done to merit a visit from the mother of my Lord? At the sound of your voice, the child in my womb leapt for joy! Happy are you because you have believed that what the Lord said to you will come to pass. You are the most blessed of all women, and blessed is the Fruit of your womb."

Moved by the same Spirit, Mary replied:

"Sing, my soul, the greatness of the Lord! Be happy, my spirit, in God, my Savior. Tenderly has He dealt with His servant, lowly though she is. From this day, ages to come will call me blessed."

Her song thanked and praised the Lord for His blessings on her and her cousin and on everyone! Their happiness represented the fulfillment of impossible yearnings and dreams, impossible for men and women but not for their Creator, whose love knows no bounds.

Mary's song echoed an ancient paean of praise on the lips of Anna, in the days of the Judges, a thousand years before. Do you remember?"

I did but asked to him tell that story handed on by word of mouth and the pen of a scribe. As he did, a thousand years faded away:

"Elkanah and his two wives, Anna and Penninah, lived in the hill country to the north of Jerusalem. Anna was barren, as Peninnah, the mother of several sons and daughters, kept reminding her. It was not a joyful time for Anna when the family made the annual pilgrimage of thanksgiving to Shiloh, at that time the religious center of our people.

One year, Anna had had enough! Elkanah had offered the sacrifice to the Lord and distributed shares to his family. The fruitful wife received several shares but Anna only one. She prayed to the Lord, promising if He gave her a son to give him back in sacred service.

The Lord listened and blessed her womb; the next time she slept with Elkanah she conceived and bore a son. She named him Samuel, "asked of the Lord," and brought him as a lad to Shiloh, to dedicate him to the Lord's service, as she had promised. She was filled with the Spirit, singing.

"My heart is happy in the Lord. In Him I hold my head high... Cease your boasting...The barren woman is fruitful, but the mother of many is left to languish."

Samuel grew to be leader of Israel, the last of its Judges. As he advanced in age he heeded the popular demand for a king and anointed Saul. When Saul's devotion declined, Samuel chose David, a young shepherd of Bethlehem, to be the messiah, the anointed one. David was ancestor to Joseph, Mary's husband and legal father to Jesus.

To return to the scene at the village of vineyards, the happiness felt by Mary and Elizabeth was as real as it was mysterious. Unable to explain their joy, they simply sang and laughed together!

Three months later, on a dry midsummer day a child was born to the elderly couple. Mary stayed until the day set for the circumcision and naming of the boy. Elizabeth would need her supportive presence that day. When the day arrived, relatives and friends gathered. The still speechless Zachary had communicated to Elizabeth the command of the Lord to name the boy,"John." When she announced his name the relatives and friends objected; it was a name unknown in the family. Turning to her husband for help, she asked him to write the boy's name for all to see. He wrote, "his name is John."

At this, the old man's tongue was loosed. He began to sing, in solemn tones of Temple music. The gathered guests neither understood nor questioned the clearly inspired words that sing of God's fulfilling the promisesHe made to His people over the centuries. Zachary sees his own son's birth as a herald of an age of fulfillment. Mary's memory recorded them, and as I remember them:

"Blessed be the God of Israel! He has visited His people and set them free. He has raised up a mighty Savior of the house of His servant, David, as He promised through His holy prophets, that He would deliver us from our enemies...And you, my child...will go ahead of the Lord, to prepare His way...The sun of salvation will rise upon us, to shine on those who live in darkness...to guide us in the way of peace."

Contention ceased. The celebration commenced! Everyone began to sing and play their drums and pipes. Mary left for Nazareth on the following day. It was now six months, and her Child was growing heavy. Yet her heart was light as she bade her cousins farewell.

The Birth of Jesus the Christ

That year the winter was mild, fortunately for Mary and Joseph. It was a year of census, and heads of families had to register in their place of birth. For Joseph, as I've said, this was the little village of Bethlehem, just south of the Holy City. He had gone north to the more prosperous Galilee, but his relatives were still near the town of their ancestor, David the King. The family pedigree was royal, but its actual state quite modest, bordering on poverty. It was a good occasion for Joseph to take Mary and introduce her to his relatives..

Bethlehem was small, and its houses small, unable to provide rooms for those returning there to register. Mary's health was robust, but she was due to give birth very soon. She went with Joseph, but very slowly. By the time they reached Bethlehem, the tiny town was filled. There was no room for them in the inn.

Near the inn was a grotto, one of the many in the area, used as a stable. It was there, in the middle of the night, that Mary gave birth to a Child, the Son promised her. Following God's word, she named her baby, "Jesus," that is, "Savior."

At this point, the old man paused and looked into the sky. He seemed to be addressing the world but spoke softly:

"This is mystery, beyond the limits of the human mind: God became one of us! In His Son, God bridged the unbridgeable gap between the human and the divine.

The cry of the newborn Child was the cry of the human race, and it was the cry of God! Without losing His divine nature, the Son of God assumed our human nature. For us, God became poor, begging for our love. His final word begins with the weak wail of the Baby and concludes with the faint whisper of the Man dying on the cross, soon to rise again."

I waited while he looked out over the City, as if he once again saw the Child become a man, dying in agony, risen in glory. Still staring at the city across the valley, he continued the story of the birth in Bethlehem:

"Outside, there were shepherds watching their flocks in the fields. They were not highly regarded by the "religious" people, because these rough shepherds were illiterate and had only minimal schooling in Scripture. Above all, their work kept them from attending regular worship in the Temple. Since He too was kept outside the world He created, God felt at ease with these simple souls. They were the first He told of the birth of His Son.

The glory of God appeared to these outsiders, transforming a starless sky into a luminous space. The heavens shook and became bright with light. The shepherds were afraid, but an angel called to them:

"Don't be afraid. I have good news for you, joy to the world. This day a Savior, Christ the Lord, is born, here in the town of David. See for yourselves. You'll find a baby wrapped in swaddling clothes and lying in a manger."

Then the heavens filled with great choirs of angels singing, "glory to God in the highest! Peace on earth to men and women God loves."

As the vision vanished, the youngest shepherd said, "let's go and see!"

The old man stopped speaking. After some minutes, he said:

"Forgive me. I'm quite distracted. You see, this youngest shepherd was the one who described the vision of God's glory to me. He died just recently. It was surely no accident that he and all those simple shepherds, or those who were still living when Jesus taught here in Jerusalem became His followers.

I knew them all."

Coming back to his story, he continued:

"The other shepherds agreed and walked through the fields to the inn at the outskirts of the little town. As they neared the place, this simple

10

youth asked, with a wisdom beyond his years and status, "could this be King Messiah, the Son of David?"

God knew, if I might so speak, to whom He was confiding the news of the birth of His Son in time. These simple sons of Israel knew of the prophetic promise: a messiah would rise from David's descendants, a king to save and rule Israel.

Reaching the cave used as a stable, they fell to their knees in worship and wonder. As these simple shepherds offered the first homage of the human race to its newborn King, Mary too was wrapped in wonder. The shepherds left, Mary and her Child slept, and the world around them slumbered on.

Eight days later, Mary and Joseph took the Child to be circumcised and given His name: Jesus, that is, Savior. As they presented Him in the Temple, an aged man named Simeon came up to them. He had waited his life long for the salvation of Israel. The Spirit had promised him that he would not die before seeing the fulfillment of his longing. Guided by this same Spirit He had come to the Temple. Taking the Child in his arms, he prayed:

"Now, Lord, You may let Your servant go in peace. I have seen with my own eyes Your salvation, a light for the Gentiles and glory for Your people, Israel."

Mary and Joseph were still pondering the old man's words when an elderly prophetess named Anna came up. She too praised the Lord for the Child. To all who would listen she spoke of His saving mission. In fact, no one but His parents paid much attention. As the Light of the world left the Temple, the shadows began to spread, barely held back by the great Temple torches.

The Magi

Far to the east, beyond the Jordan river and the vast lands of the desert, wisdom's light appeared to other "outsiders." Divine wisdom finds a place in any pure heart. Jew or Gentile, Christian or pagan.

The one and the same God sends His Spirit into any receptive soul. Jewish shepherds saw the glory of the Lord over Bethlehem, and Gentile Magi saw the light of His star in the East, from their home in in Babylon.

Fabled Babylon! Pearl of the East. Filled with palaces, palm trees and lush green gardens, it stretched along the banks of the great river Euphrates. Enlivened by merchants and scholars of many nations. Among the scholars were scribes of our Jewish people. They studied and transmitted sacred traditions. Among the Gentile scholars were Magi, Persian priests who study dreams of the mind and stars of the sky.

Excited by this brightest of stars, the Magi consulted the other scholars of the sacred. Since a new star appears at the birth of each person, whose star was this? Whose birth did it announce, this star outshining all others?

An elderly Hebrew scribe answered:

"It must be the star of Jacob. Balaam of old prophesied that a star would rise from Jacob to defeat the enemies of Israel, the children of Jacob."

The scribe went on to say:

"How high above us are the ways of the Lord! As He once spoke through Balaam, a Gentile priest and prophet, now He has spoken to us through you Gentile priests. As once He blessed His people, Israel, through the Gentile Balaam, may He now bless us through you."

"What should we do?" they asked.

"Follow the star. It shines in the west, over the land of Israel. Go there, enquire of the Scribes in our Holy City. Ask to see the newborn King. Start as soon as you can, today, tomorrow, but go, follow that light!"

That same day, as darkness fell, three of the Magi did set out, led by the light of the star. Resting by day, riding at night, they arrived in Jerusalem and asked:

"Where is the newborn King of the Jews?"

With the speed usual to our little cities, the news spread and stirred the Holy City. The actual king of the Jews, Herod, was far from pleased and sent for the Magi.

Nearing the end of his days, the crafty ruler was as suspicious as ever. In his paranoia, he had murdered even his own sons and his favorite wife! Assuring the Magi of his support, he summoned learned priests and scribes, the most knowledgeable of all who studied the Scriptures. He asked:

"Where will the Messiah be born?"

"In Bethlehem of Judah," they replied. They cited the prophecy of Micah:

"You, Bethlehem, are by no means the least important town of Judah, for from you will come a leader who will guide My people Israel."

Deceitfully, Herod invited the Magi to return and let him know where they found the Child, so he too might go and worship Him. They expressed their gratitude to the royal scoundrel for his help but firmly refused an escort. They had to reach their goal by themselves. At sunset they began the final stage of their journey, still guided by the light of the star. It led them to the humble home that now lodged the holy pair and their Child.

Kneeling in homage, the Magi offered gifts of gold, frankincense, and myrrh. Then they left to pitch their tents outside the town.

Mary kept the memory of this additional mystery in her heart all her life. When she had received the Spirit after Jesus' ascent into glory she saw the significance of the gifts. She told me: gold for His kingship, incense for His divinity, and myrrh, used at death, for His humanity.

The sudden appearance of these Gentile priests on the stage of our history reminds me of the equally mysterious appearance of a Gentile priest in the history of Abraham, the father of our race: Melchizedek, the Gentile priest-king of Jerusalem long before it became David's capital, came out to meet Abraham with bread and wine as an offering to his God to celebrate Abraham's victory over his enemies. Abraham gave him a share of the booty and was blessed by the priest-king. Then, Melchizedek disappeared from history, leaving no trace behind him.

The Magi likewise vanished into the desert, leaving no footprints behind them. Before they did, they had a dream. God warned them not to return to Herod. Heeding His word, they rose and departed before dawn, while the restless king still tossed and turned.

Finding no sleep, he got out of bed and spent the rest of the time till sunrise perfecting his plan. He would trick the Magi into revealing where they found the Child. He waited all that day, but it passed as had the Magi. Furious, he sent men to Bethlehem with orders to kill every male child of two years and under.

Joseph too had had a dream; he was warned to flee with Mary and the Child. They fled to Egypt and remained there till they heard of Herod's death.

Jesus in the Temple

Twelve years later found Mary and Joseph back in Nazareth. At Passover time they went up to the Holy City with a group of pilgrims. At the end of the Feast they began their homeward journey. A whole day had gone by before they realized Jesus was not with them. Filled with the fear felt by parents of a missing child, Mary and Joseph returned to Jerusalem and began their search. They found Jesus in the Temple, sitting in the midst of teachers and answering their questions, as if He were the rabbi!

Mary asked Him:

"Why did You do this to us? Your father and I have been so worried."

"Why were you worried? Did you not know I would be in My Father's house?"

His answer left Mary and Joseph all the more perplexed, but Jesus went back with them to Nazareth and was obedient to them. He grew into a gifted and attractive young man. The world next heard of Him when He appeared at the banks of the Jordan river, where John was baptizing with water as a sign of the repentance he was preaching.

JESUS BAPTIZED AND TEMPTED

Jesus was about thirty years old when He appeared at the Jordan river.

John was there, preaching repentance and baptizing. This gaunt ascetic embodied the radical attitude he preached. His clothing was the simplest, of camel hair with a leather belt around his waist. For food he ate locusts and wild honey. Stripping his body of all but essentials he could focus on the voice speaking to his soul.

This divine voice ordered John to leave his desert and preach the need for change of heart. He was to turn men and women back towards their God, to proclaim and prepare the way for the One to come. The One to come would take away the sin of the world, that is, the mysterious but real alienation of the human race from its God.

The sign of inner cleansing and change of heart was baptism in water of the Jordan river, the river that marks the boundary between the wilderness and the Promised Land. Crowds flocked to hear John and be baptized.

When Jesus appeared on the scene, John's pure heart and unencumbered mind perceived what others could not: Jesus' true identity. John sensed, as he had sensed in his mother's womb, the presence of holiness, of the divine. The reaction of the voiceless baby in the womb had been to leap with joy. Now grown to manhood, and again moved by the Spirit, John's reaction was to say to his disciples:

"There is the Lamb of God, who will take away the sin of the world."

To John's amazement and confusion, the spotless Lamb came to him and asked to be baptized. John protested:

"You come to me? I should be baptized by You!"

The Lamb answered:

"Let it be as I ask. Let justice be satisfied."

I interrupted the older disciple to ask:

"What does this mean?"

15

The wise old disciple hesitated a few seconds before he spoke slowly, trying to make it simple for me, He continued:

"In our tradition justice is a harmony between God's plan for us and the actual situation. When things are as they ought to be, as God wants them to be, then justice prevails. Because we are unable by ourselves to restore justice, the harmony between God and the human race, God sent His Son to be one of us, to represent us. He was baptized not because He needed it but because we do; in His accepting baptism Jesus formally acknowledged that He was a member, a part of our human family.

Jesus now knew He was to begin the work for which He been sent. He was to justify us. We are "justified" when God forgives us our sins. John's baptism asked God to forgive sins. The baptism you and all followers of Christ receive actually does forgive sins, because of Him.

While the water still dripped from Jesus' head, He heard the voice of His heavenly Father, assuring Him of His love:

"You are My beloved Son."

His Father was acknowledging Jesus as His Son, pledging His guidance and support. When we are baptized He acknowledges us as His adopted children. We were all born once into this life, but with our baptism we are born again, this time into God's divine life! It is the gateway by which we enter into His life.

Jesus then saw the Holy Spirit descend on Him as a dove, symbol of peace and reconciliation. and of the choice of Jesus as God's prophet, one who speaks for Him. We too are chosen to be God's prophets, speaking for Him, of course only in and through Christ.

The Temptation

After His baptism, Jesus was tempted, as we are, by the devil. These temptations concern the choices a human person has to make between the material, that passes, and the spiritual, that lasts.

He was led by the Spirit into the desert, favored abode of the devil. The devil hates anything that can make us happy, and the desert has very little to make us happy. There are good spirits that urge us to turn towards God, and there are evil spirits, devils, that urge us to turn away from God and from the happiness He wants to share with us.

Sometimes we give a name to the chief devil, "Satan," which means one who accuses, who takes the part of the prosecuting lawyer. The Spirit of God takes the role of the attorney for our defense! He urges us to trust in God's love for us. The Spirit was always with Jesus, unseen but always nearby.

Jesus remained in the wilderness for forty days, fasting. The number "forty" in our tradition signifies a life span. For forty years our ancestors wandered in the wilderness. We too wander in the wilderness of this life for our "forty years," our span of years.

Freed from the bondage of Egypt, our forebears passed through the water of the Red Sea. The water saved them from recapture or even death. Freed from slavery to sin, we pass through the water of baptism that saves us from death. They were on their way to the Promised Land. We are on our way to the land promised us, God's own home.

In the first of three temptations, the devil urged Jesus to assuage His hunger:

"If You are the Son of God, command these stones to turn into bread!"

Jesus did not deny the body's need for food, but answering the devil He spoke of food that nourishes the spirit for eternal life. The divine guidance, the Torah, given to our ancestors to follow was often spoken of as food for the spirit. The spirit lasts into eternity, whereas the body dies within a span of years. Jesus answered the tempter:

"Humans do not live by bread alone but by every word that comes from the mouth of God."

Next, the devil transported Jesus to the pinnacle of the Temple. High above the rocky slope, which you can still see there; a fall would mean the end of this life. The day would come when Jesus would be taunted:

"If You are the Son of God, come down from the cross!"

Now in the desert, the devil tempted Jesus to a material show of His power:

"If You are the Son of God, throw Yourself down, for Scripture says: God will order His angels to hold you up with their hands, lest you hurt your feet on the stones."

Jesus countered:

"Scripture also says: do not put the Lord your God to the test."

Finally, the devil placed Jesus on a great height, showing Him the mighty kingdoms of the world, and he said:

"I will give all these to You, if You kneel and adore me!"

At this claim to worship, due to God alone, Jesus banished the devil:

"Be gone, Satan. It is written: you shall worship the Lord your God and Him alone shall you serve."

Jesus would show He is Son of God by His love, giving His life for ours. His death for our life, as His Father asked. You and I show God is our Father not by the wonders we might work but by the love we live. Satan left Jesus, and His Father sent angels to restore Him, to get Him ready for the start of His public ministry.

We've spoken of the temptations Jesus endured and overcame for us. You know that the basic notion of being tempted is that of being tested and tried. Jesus was tested and tried. His faith, His love for His Father and for us was tested at the very beginning of His ministry. Jesus replied for all of us to the complaint of God to our ancestors that they had tested His love for them!

In a beautiful psalm come down to us from our forebears, His chosen people of old, God had complained. Now usually the psalms express the moods of the human heart, faith, fear, gratitude... In this psalm God does the talking and tells His people they're not appreciative of all He has done for them. He reminds them of the forty years in the wilderness when all they did was test and try Him. Did He really love them? Did He care for them? Was He truly their God?

Jesus answered for all of us in this testing of His faith and His love. He would face many more tests and finally triumph over death itself, for us, as one of us.

Our forebears had faith that a Messiah (anointed king) would come and represent God's people in doing battle with their enemies, emerging victorious from the wilderness, restoring the primeval harmony that had existed between humankind and the wild beasts. Jesus identified himself as the long awaited Messiah.

Death of the Baptist

The passing of the torch from the herald to the Healer occurred soon after Jesus returned to Galilee. He began Himself to preach and to heal when He heard John had been thrown into prison by Herod Antipas. Antipas was the son of the Herod who'd sought Jesus' death soon after His birth in Bethlehem. John denounced Antipas for marrying the wife of his own brother, who was still alive.

From prison, John sent word to Jesus:

"Are You the One who is to come?"

Jesus' reply assured the prisoner that his own mission had been fulfilled. John's messengers were told to tell him what they heard and saw: the sick were healed, and the poor had the good news preached to them. Jesus had a special word for His forerunner:

"Happy are they who have no doubts about Me!"

John repeated to his faithful followers what he had already said of his relationship to the One who was to come:

"He must increase. I must decrease."

Within a few days he departed this life, murdered by Herod. That king's wife had found an occasion to rid herself and her husband of the troublesome Prophet; it was at Herod's birthday celebration. Herod's stepdaughter, Salome, so enchanted him with her dancing that he promised her anything she wished as reward. Consulting her mother, she asked for the head of John the Baptist. That very day the light of the forerunner blended into the light of the One who had come.

HAPPINESS

Spring had spread her green carpet on the hills where Jesus had grown to manhood. One fresh morning we climbed the grassy slope of a hill overlooking the lake, a few minutes' walk from Capharnaum. Jesus was sitting there waiting. When He spoke it was of life, of happiness.

I was young, but I was aware that this life is passing. From time to time I even pondered the fact that this life cannot satisfy my desire for a happiness that neither ends nor disappoints. In spite of this, I kept on living in a materialistic manner; I wanted satisfaction here and now. That morning Jesus opened the eyes of my soul. I wanted the life He promised!

The life He promised is not the life we now live but the life to come, a share in God's own life! The root of my happiness is the realization that God wants each of us to share this divine life. Even now,

I'm happy not only when the sun shines on me but also when things are bleak or worse, when I think of what He has in store for those who love Him and hope in Him. Yes, my joy is not always all that evident to myself or to others, but it is so deeply embedded in my heart that it comes to the surface more quickly than I'm sure it would if I had no faith in the life to come.

This belief in a better life to come is of course part of our Jewish heritage. Most of our people believe in the resurrection of body and soul. This belief came about gradually, for the older belief of our people considered the grave as leading at best to a shadowy form of existence that was not too attractive. That's why many looked to every sort of pleasure and power this life can give.

This spring day Jesus spoke especially to those who seemed to be losing the struggle to be happy.

The blessings, the beatitudes, He promised are those of the life to come.

The Beatitudes

No one wrote down the exact words of Jesus. It was not the only time He answered the basic question of the human heart, how can I be happy? That morning, however, the setting and weather were so beautiful and memorable that many of us simply thought of this occasion whenever we did recall the theme, how to be happy.

Jesus said:

"Happy are the poor in spirit. Yours is the kingdom of God.

Happy are those who are hungry now. You will be filled.

Happy are those who weep now. One day you will laugh!

Happy are you when you're hated, and rejected, and slandered, because of Me. Your reward will be great in heaven."

Then He reminded us of the transitory nature of this life and all its material blessings:

"Alas for you who are rich now. You've had your blessing.

Alas for you who are full now. One day, you'll be hungry

Alas for you who hear everyone speaking well of you. Your forebears spoke well of false prophets."

These woes were not curses. Jesus was expressing, in our Semitic way, the dilemma: how can we yearn for things that last if we're satisfied with things that pass away? We see that this life does come to an end. It has to lead to something beyond....

I remember three more blessings Jesus announced that day, or at least I and others think of them as having been given that same day:

"Happy are the humble. You will possess the Land.

Happy are the merciful. You will be treated with mercy.

Happy are the pure of heart. You will see God!"

Remember that in our Hebrew tradition to see God is to be with Him. The pure of heart see God because there is nothing in their hearts to obscure their vision. They see Him because their hearts are like His. They know when He is near and recognize His voice when He speaks. On God's part we know He must be most comfortable with a pure heart, a heart that mirrors His own!

Jesus said:

"Happy are the peacemakers. You will be called children of God."

Remember that peace is another word for justice, the state of harmony that exists between God and His people. It cannot exist in our hearts if we are unjust in our relationships with one another. Justice and peace depend on our being humble. In fact, all of these beatitudes are aspects of the one beatitude, "happy are the humble. They will inherit the Land."

To be humble, to inherit the Land. I see by your face that I should explain the two ideas.

Perhaps you are not familiar with a tradition that developed among our rabbis at the same time as their coming to believe in the resurrection? Although the destruction of our Temple and this city shook the faith of many, some still believe today that the resurrection will take place in the Land, that is this land where we now are, for some it's just Jerusalem. Therefore at the resurrection all the upright will come here to receive the reward of their struggle to be faithful to the Law of the Lord. This is what Jesus had in mind when He promised the humble, the meek, they would inherit the land, but of course we now believe that the land promised us is heaven itself, the place where God "rests," i.e., dwells.

To be humble. Jesus is the best example of that that means! Therefore...

"Learn from Me"

The notion of humility, of being humble and meek, is much misunderstood. Great minds of the Gentiles commonly taught that humility is not to be cultivated, for they considered it simply a giving way to others and thus a loss of esteem both in our own eyes and in those of others. Jesus showed the true nature of humility when He said: Learn from Me, for I am gentle and humble of heart, and you will find rest for your souls.

Humility brings us peace of soul because it is most natural for a human person to know that we are dependent it is also natural to have a concern for the needs of others. Jesus is the model for the humble person because He came into our world out of concern for our need to be reconciled with our God, and He constantly showed His loving dependence on His Father in heaven. A great sign of His care for us is His mercy. He personified the beatitude, "happy are the merciful."

The humble person is merciful, seeing others as God sees them. To be humble is to see not only our dependence on God but also to be filled with gratitude for His love for all of us, no matter how imperfect and seemingly unlovable we may be to a merely human vision. The humble, the merciful, and the pure of heart all focus their attention on God and His loving plan for each of us.

The Little Ones

Jesus often spoke of the little ones, the dependent ones, the children, the poor. One of the most firmly established traditions of our people is the care of the poor. Among the books of Wisdom one of Jesus' favorites was the Wisdom of Sirach. After many years of travel and close observation of human nature this sage opened a school in Jerusalem to teach the young how to truly live and to be happy. He taught, among the hundreds of wise counsels, that to harm or even neglect the poor is most offensive to God, for, "the prayer of the poor pierces the clouds; it goes straight to God's heart."

Although the Son of God owns the universe He became poor for the sake of the human race, for the sake of each of us. He was born poor, and He died poor, because of His love for us. There is an image of this Man of Nazareth on the face of every person who is poor. There the Father sees the face of His Son. Remember the teaching of our ancient book of Proverbs, the oldest of our Wisdom books:

When you are kind to the poor, you are lending to God, and God himself will repay you!

Although I am speaking here of the materially poor, we know that everyone is poor in spirit, needing the practical concern of others who act as channels of God's care for them. Those with more material goods are also chosen channels of God's concern for the poor, and at the end of time these little ones will be witnesses on behalf of those who have shared with them.

I remember Jesus identifying Himself with the poor in material things and the poor in spirit, for He once said that whenever we help the thirsty and the hungry and the poorly clothed and visit the sick and the imprisoned, all these "little ones," dependent in some way on our kindness, we do it all to Him!

Children of course combine both a need and an openness to be helped, and they are more trusting by nature. A child knows its need and trusts that an older person will help. Jesus loved to have them around! They revived His spirit on hard days, those days when His message seemed to fall on deaf ears. I recall one of those days.

It was towards evening of a long day of preaching and healing. Everyone was tired. Then some women appeared with their babies and toddlers, asking Jesus to bless them. The weary disciples told them to go away, but Jesus said:

"Don't keep them from Me. The kingdom of heaven belongs to little ones."

He took each little one in His arms and blessed it.

I remember another time when some of the disciples, including myself, were arguing about who was the most important! Jesus was entertaining some children when He heard us and called us over to hear His judgment:

"The most important one is this child. Unless you become like little children, you will not enter the Kingdom."

The Kingdom

God is spirit, so His kingdom, His dominion, is spiritual. Jesus had to remind us of this more than once. He distinguished its sphere from the kingdoms of this world and their civil authority. The spiritual transcends the limits of individual nations and peoples. The kingdom of God is open to everyone who accepts God's invitation to share His life.

This was new indeed. Many could not or would not understand that Jesus had come as a non-political Messiah. Rejecting His message, some of the clever ones laid a trap for Him. It was in Galilee, not far from the city of Tiberias on the shore of the sea of Galilee.

They paid some roving actors to pretend they were pious Jews asking Jesus for a rabbinic decision.

His judgment would either arouse the ruling Roman authority or alienate patriotic Jews. In either case He would be in trouble. By the way, in those days before the great revolt of our people against the Roman occupiers of our land the theater was frowned upon as a mark of Greek culture, hostile to our Jewish culture. Actors were either Gentiles or non-observant Jews. They spoke Greek, as did most Galileans. Jesus of course knew this language but usually spoke in His native Aramaic.

Speaking in Aramaic now, the actors said:

"Rabbi, we know You are a just man who is not influenced by a person's status. Give us your opinion. Should we pay tribute to Caesar?"

The Reader of hearts discerned the mask of the actor and replying in Greek said:

"Hypocrites. Show Me a coin." A hypocrite, remember, is one playing a role.

When they showed Him a coin He asked:

"Whose name and face are on the coin?"

They answered:

"Caesar's"

Jesus rendered His decision:

"Then give to Caesar what is Caesar's. Give to God what is God's"

Some Parables

Jesus was a great story teller, as many of our people still are. He saw that stories attracted attention, and that most of us remember a story better than the original sermon! The parables Jesus used to make His point are quite similar to the fables Greeks use to convey a message. Of course everything that is passed on by word of mouth changes a bit in the telling, and a few of Jesus' parables are puzzling to us, even to me, for the original point Jesus made has been forgotten! Most of His parables are very easily understood, however. They stay in our minds.

Soon after Jesus' sermon that morning He noticed different reactions and told a parable to show the diverse ways of receiving His word. we now call this parable the parable of the sower:

"A sower sowed seeds in various types of soil. The first was a beaten track. The seed lay there a few minutes. Then birds came and took it.

The sower also sowed on thin soil. The heat of the sun and the rain caused the seed to quickly sprout, but it also quickly died in the shallow soil.

The third type of soil to receive the seed was rocky. Thorns and thistles outgrew the plants and choked the life out of them.

The sower sowed most promisingly in deep and fertile soil. Growing slowly but firmly the seed developed into pleasant and fruitful plants."

Asking themselves if they had correctly interpreted the parable some disciples asked Jesus to give them His explanation, so He told us:

"The seed is the word of God. The soil is the heart of the hearer. Some pay no attention at all. Others do but are flighty by nature or only listen out of curiosity. Some are sincere but let worries and fears control their lives. Finally, there are those who treat the word of God as a deep well from which water can be drawn, in good times and in times of drought."

Jesus spoke of the central place the Kingdom should have in our thinking and in our planning. The Kingdom is where God dwells, where He is, the place He "rests," as our ancient Hebrew tradition has expressed it. Of course we only fully enjoy this Kingdom when we pass from this life to the life He promises us if we are faithful, to the life that will never end. Even now, however, we can have a taste of the joy to come when we open the door of our hearts to Him, to come in and be with us! This door of course is love. Even those who do not know Him by name enjoy His presence, an ineffable feeling of peace, whenever we do something kind for another.

Jesus could speak of the Kingdom of God among us, for the Kingdom being God's presence, Jesus was this divine presence. That's why He spoke of Himself as the Temple. To think of God's humility, to come among us as another man. We touched Him. We ate and drank with Him and we laughed with Him, God among us. How wondrous!

More Parables

Jesus told a parable to remind us that we have to begin now, at this very moment, to invite Him into our lives and not to wait until the day we die. It's the parable of the rich man and the poor man. Jesus gave the poor man a name, Eliezer, which means, remember, in our Hebrew tongue, "God is my helper." This name is a promising one, to keep another of our old Jewish traditions according to which a great book is kept in heaven with the names of those who will live there forever. Jesus's love for the poor reflected His Father's, and He loved to promise ultimate victory for the little ones, those so often seen as losing the struggles of this life.

I know that this parable is a great favorite with the church in Rome, where you give the rich man the symbolic name of Dives, your Latin word for "rich." You also translate "Eliezer" into your Latin, "Lazarus." Well, to get on with this beautiful parable...

"There was a rich man who feasted and dressed for each day as if it were a great feast day. He was not a cruel man, but neither was he a humble man, a kind man, caring for the needs of others.

A poor man named Lazarus sat at Dives' gate. No one cared for him; Dives passed him many times, pretending not to see him. Dogs, however, took pity on him, licking his festering sores. He died alone but was carried by angels to join our father Abraham at the feast that never ends. Dives too died and was buried with great pomp; he was assigned a place in Hades. From his place of torment he could see Lazarus resting in the bosom of Abraham. He called to him:

"Father Abraham. Send Lazarus to dip his hand in water and cool my tongue. This fire is terrible!"

"My son, remember that you had everything you wanted on earth, while Lazarus had nothing. Besides, between you and us thee is an uncrossable abyss."

"Then send Lazarus to warn my brothers."

"They have Moses and the Prophets. Let them listen to their teaching."

"No, Father Abraham. If only someone would rise from the dead...."

"If they ignore Moses and the Prophets, they will pay no attention to One who rises from the dead."

We know from what we see that, as an inspired poet has said, "our days are like a flower, the wind comes and it is gone, its place now empty."

Our Scriptures also tell us that the rich cannot pay a ransom for their lives, that they take nothing with them when they die. With this in mind, Jesus told another parable on the importance of imitating God in His kindness in this life to be at ease with Him and welcomed by Him to share His life when we pass from this earthly existence:

"Ten virgins were chosen to light the way for a bridegroom on his wedding night. Five were wise, and five were improvident. They were all waiting with lamps lighted for the bridegroom but fell asleep when his coming was delayed. Suddenly they heard the shout:

"The bridegroom's coming! Get ready."

The five wise virgins refilled their lamps with the extra oil they had brought along, but the other five had not thought of this and now begged the wise virgins to lend them some oil.

"We can't lend you any, for then there might not be enough for all of us. Best go and get some."

The unhappy women hurried off to find some oil. Meanwhile, the bridegroom arrived and went into the banquet with the five wise virgins. The other five arrived to find the door closed.

"Open for us," they called in to the bridegroom.

"I don't know you," he called back.

Jesus added: be watchful. You know neither the day nor the hour.

I could add here that the soothing quality of oil makes it a symbol of doing good deeds for others.

From time to time we realize we have had an unkind first reaction to another person and then spend too long regretting this. Jesus addressed this very subject with a little parable:

"A man had two sons. He asked them to go and work in his field. One said, "yes," but did not go. The other said, "no, I won't go," but then repented and did go. An initial unkindness is erased from God's memory by our repentance and efforts to be kind in thought and deed.

There is something similar in another little parable Jesus told to teach us that God is patient with us in this life:

"A man planted good seed in a field. During the night someone came and sowed bad seed in that field. When the grain appeared, so did the weeds. The man's workers asked what happened. The man replied that an enemy did this.

"Shall we take out the weeds?"

"No, you might damage the good grain. Wait till harvest time. Then we will separate the grain from the weeds."

My Happiness

Among the love songs of our people, the Psalms express the deepest emotions of the human heart. In these love songs God is sometimes praised and sometimes questioned (scolded). In psalm 73 the poet complains that God allows the ruthless rich and powerful to do as they please, to act as gods with no respect for others, all of whom have been made in the image of God. In prayer He receives God's answer and can only share the joy of his heart at the conviction that he has nothing in heaven or on earth but God. He exclaims: To be near God is my happiness!

Jesus told a parable to remind us to pause and ponder our notion of ultimate happiness. What is the most precious thing in my life?

"A merchant dealing in fine gems found a pearl of surpassing beauty. At last, the perfect pearl! He sold everything he had to make it his."

He expressed the same thought in a slightly different way:

"Another man discovered a treasure hidden in a field. He buried it and sold everything he had to buy that field."

What lies ahead?

After this life fades from sight, is that the end? Jesus encountered people who thought so, who even opposed His teaching that for those who are loving persons death is a door leading to an incomparably more beautiful life. Among His most bitter opponents was a small but powerful group of our people, the Sadducees. They have since disappeared as an influential group, since the priestly families formed the core of this group, and of course their priestly function ceased with the destruction of the Temple.

The Sadducees were mostly from families of considerable wealth and extremely conservative. They accepted only the older books of our Scriptures as inspired by God; they rejected the commonly held belief among our people of a gradual unfolding of God's revelation to us. Of course they refused to even consider Jesus as the ultimate and living word of God! His followers believe He guides us still.

Since the belief in the resurrection was not clearly stated in the older books and can only be seen in later books of Scripture the Sadducees would not believe it. To show the absurdity of Jesus' teaching on the resurrection they asked Him to answer this question:

"A woman's husband died before she conceived, so to raise up children to the family's name she married his brother, as Moses commanded. This man also died before his wife could conceive and the same happened to five other brothers. Which one would be her husband in the life to come?"

Jesus reminded these scoffers that their God is the God of the living, that the deceased Abraham and Isaac and Jacob were thought to be still living, though not present when God appeared to Moses and said: I am the God of Abraham, Isaac, and Jacob. Therefore there must be a resurrection, for this encounter of Moses with the Lord, the God of Israel at the burning bush was recounted by Moses himself, according to the Sadducees' own belief!

Furthermore, the life to come is far beyond the limits of this life and of our understanding, for it is God's ow divine life. There are no limits to love, to happiness in heaven. God has placed this desire for happiness within our hearts. This is our faith. It is what lies ahead....

HIS DISCIPLES

Near the ninth hour of the following day, we were again on the hillside, waiting. There was freshness in the air and hope in our hearts. Responding to our need, Jesus began to teach:

"Come to Me, you who are weary and find life hard to bear. Take My yoke and learn from Me. I am gentle and humble of heart. You will find peace of soul. My yoke is pleasant. My load is light."

I craved this peace of soul. This peace that is the rest God promised our ancestors as they wandered in the wilderness. It is a taste on earth of the peace one day to be ours forever. Jesus was giving us His torah, His guidance, to light our way.

As I listened on that hillside I thought:

"He's a new Moses!"

Moses had been the channel of God's torah for our forebears. As a lamp to light their steps on their way through life God gave them His torah through Moses on the heights of Mount Sinai. Sinai's soaring peaks seem to pierce the sky, reaching up to meet the Lord. Moses did go up this mountain to meet the Lord, while the people waited in fear at its foot.

In Jesus, God came down Himself to meet His people. On the gentle sloping hillside and later on the plain at its foot, Jesus gave His Father's torah to all who would listen. This time, God did not speak in the roar of fire and thunder on the top of the mighty mountain but in a gentle voice speaking of peace.

When Jesus compared His torah to a yoke He was following a common rabbinic practice. Oxen bear a yoke to direct their way. Rabbis recalled that we freely accept God's torah to direct our way.

All teachers transmit something of themselves to disciples. They pass on to them their personal view of a text or tradition. Kind persons see things in a kindly light. Harsh persons share their harshness. Religion is no exception!

Loving persons pass on their vision of a loving God. Severe men and women share their vision of a God who is demanding and at times unforgiving. To convey a true image and reflection of Himself, God sent His Son, Jesus the Christ. In Him, God teaches His torah, directly.

Unlike all other teachers, including Moses, Jesus taught with God's own voice. In His torah, there is no merely human vision.

I found much to ponder in Jesus' words, "My load is light."

First of all, I remember Jesus complaining, on more than one occasion, to teachers of torah. He said their harshness was placing a heavy burden on the shoulders of the simple folk who tried to follow God's law. Then, I myself was not traveling light but with too much baggage! Besides resentments and things I was sure I needed, I was weighed down by the gold in my purse and the self in my soul!

I'll tell you now of the call of certain disciples by Jesus and their response. These are from the memories of what I saw and heard myself or from what others told me.

The Twelve

On this hill He favored, Jesus formed the core of His community. He chose and set apart twelve men, Galileans like Himself, to be apostles. He would send them, as He had been sent, to proclaim the Kingdom of God. The twelve apostles were to be the nucleus of Israel renewed, as the twelve sons of Jacob were the nucleus of ancient Israel. As you well know, "twelve" is a sacred number. It signifies completeness, totality.

From the beginning, Peter was their spokesman. This is what I heard of the scene of his call by Jesus:

What an extraordinary day! I was there, spending some time with my family by the lake. I witnessed some of what I'm about to relate, but Peter and my other friends filled in what I missed. I got to know Peter better, and we became close friends.

Be patient while I give you a brief background! Peter's home was at Bethsaida, farther along the shore of the lake. He had come to fish with his new partners, my friends, James and John,and their father, Zebedee. Zebedee was the husband of Salome, the sister of Jesus' mother, Mary.

James and John were thus Jesus' brothers, as Jews and Greeks both call what the Romans term "cousins." To us, every close relative is a brother or sister. These brothers of Jesus loved Him and admired Him, although other brothers were not supportive of Him until after His glorification and the sending of His Spirit. Now, to describe Peter's call, he himself told me:

It was noon, and the weather had warmed. Jesus had been teaching from Peter's boat, so He could be heard by the large number of men and women crowding the shore. After they'd gone to eat and rest, Jesus saw the empty net. He suggested they row into deeper water and lower their net for a catch. Peter said:

"We worked all night and caught nothing, but if You tell me to cast our net...."

His trust bore fruit. They caught so many fish the net was near breaking. Peter dropped to his knees and confessed his unworthiness to be Jesus' companion:

"You don't want anything to do with me! I'm a sinful man."

He knew the net filled with fish was no coincidence. It was the work of someone holy. Afraid his own unholy state would contaminate Jesus' holiness, he humbly freed Him from the bond of friendship so recently formed. Jesus assured him and the others He called that day:

"Don't worry. From now on, you'll be fishers of people!"

Jesus was accepting Peter as His friend and disciple and prophesying his future. He sometimes did this, putting a thought in our heads that remained there till the day it came about, and we remembered. By the way, I always refer to Peter by the name Jesus gave him a little later. His name at this time was still Simon, but only a few among the disciples ever used this name after Jesus' resurrection and glorification.

Peter had become Jesus' friend before this, at their first meeting. This was on the banks of the Jordan river, where John was baptizing. The Baptist had many disciples, as did all the rabbis and religious leaders, more or fewer according to their popularity! Jesus eventually aroused jealousy because of the great number of both men and women who followed Him. Peter's brother, Andrew was one of the disciples of John.

When the Baptist was divinely inspired to recognize, if only for a moment, the Lamb of God in Jesus, Andrew and another disciple asked Jesus:

"Where do You live?"

Jesus answered that they should come and see!

This was common among our people at the time, for would be disciples to go and live with the rabbi or similar personage and thus not only hear his teaching but to see him living it himself.

Andrew was most pleased with what he heard and saw, and after a brief stay with Jesus he hurried to tell his brother,

"We've found the Messiah!"

Let me tell you now how Peter received this name, even though Jesus Himself did occasionally call him, "Simon.!"

At one point in His mission Jesus withdrew from Galilee into the neighboring region of Caesarea Philippi. This was some time, later, of course. The disciples Jesus had by then formed and sent out as missionaries were to report back to Him there. When they arrived He asked them what people thought of Him. They told Him:

"Some say You're a prophet. Others say You're John the Baptist."

Jesus asked them:

"Who do you say I am?"

Peter answered:

"You are the Messiah, the Son of the Living God."

Peter realized he had spoken in the Spirit, for the words had come almost as if forced upon him. Jesus too was aware of the inspiration behind Peter's confession. He blessed him:

"Blessed are you, Simon, son of John. You will be called Peter and on this rock I'll build My church. Even the power of hell will never overcome it. I will give you the keys of the Kingdom. Whatever you bind on earth will be bound in heaven. Whatever you loose on earth will be loosed in heaven."

The new name, Cephas in Aramaic and Peter in your western tongues, signified a new role. A community was emerging that would continue after His death, for now Jesus knew He would die. I will tell you what I can remember about the call of some other disciples:

When Peter dropped everything to follow Jesus, so did his brother, Andrew, and the brothers James and John. It was to these four fishermen, really, that Jesus addressed the words:

"You'll be fishers of men."

That same day, if my memory is correct, Philip too became His disciple. He was also from Bethsaida and a friend of Peter and Andrew. He'd been a disciple of the Baptist. Friendly and outgoing, Philip enjoyed building social bridges. Many came to Jesus through him.

Philip introduced Bartholemew to Jesus. John always called him "Nathaniel," because Jesus liked the name, which means, as you know, "God's gift." John was with Jesus when Philip brought him. He told me what I'm now telling you:

Philip went to get Nathaniel and told him:

"We've found the one Moses and the Prophets spoke of! He's Jesus, son of Joseph, of Nazareth."

Nathaniel was direct, and he was blunt! He considered Nazareth too small to produce anything worthy of notice. He asked if anything worthwhile could come from Nazareth!

"Come and see for yourself," Philip countered.

When Jesus saw him, He recognized a kindred spirit, a man with an undivided heart like His own. He declared:

"Here's a true son of Israel, a man without guile."

Surprised, Nathaniel asked Him:

"How do You know me?"

Jesus answered, "I saw you sitting under the fig tree."

Nathaniel was young but wise, and he was well versed in the Scriptures of our people. He heard Jesus' words as prophecy fulfilled. Centuries before, the prophet Micah had foretold an age of peace, when a son of Israel could sit secure in the shade of his fig tree. The embodiment of this peace would be a prince of David's line, a true son of God.

"You are son of God, king of Israel." He said to Jesus.

Nathaniel was one of a long line of the pure in heart who see God. God is at ease with them and opens His heart to them. They hear secrets and revelations hidden from those who are afraid of God. Abraham, Jacob, Moses, and the Prophets all heard such things and passed them on to us.

Jesus too opened His soul to this son of Israel. He assured him:

"You'll see something greater than My prophetic gifts. Heaven will open before your eyes, and you'll see angels passing back and forth above the Son of Man."

Every Hebrew knows the dream of Jacob, our father when he slept at Bethel: he saw angels walking up and down a ladder that stretched between heaven and earth. The Jewish soul still stirs at Jacob's waking comment:

"This is truly God's house (Bethel) and the gate to heaven!"

Nathaniel was overwhelmed on hearing Jesus apply this vision to Himself. It meant that Jesus was the living ladder, the bridge between heaven and earth, the gate to heaven.

This may have been the first time Jesus called Himself the Son of Man. That mysterious figure, the son of man, appeared in the prophecy of Daniel as one sent from God but part of the human race. It was a preparation for the coming of the Son of God as a man. The title was the one I most heard Jesus use of Himself. From that day, Nathaniel became His disciple.

The Healer of Souls

The call of Levi was the most unusual. It came in Capharnaum, where Jesus had a house given Him as a center. I was in Levi's little office paying tax on my nearby property. Jesus came and looked in. It was really a meeting of minds! He said,"come, follow Me," and Levi did!

It was not as sudden as it sounds. From what he had heard of Jesus, Levi already knew Him, and Jesus knew him. Levi's younger brother, James, had become a disciple. There were two disciples named "James." We called this brother of Levi "James the Less," because he was called later than James, John's brother. Some have asked if he was shorter or younger, but I've forgotten, if I ever noticed.

Levi had wanted to be Jesus' disciple, but he held back. His occupation was to collect taxes for the foreign lords of our Land. Many considered this unclean, a blot on the holiness of the pious. The Holy One came and accepted him!

Ever ready to celebrate, Jesus held a festive meal in His house. As always, many different types of people were invited, including some of Levi's former co-workers. Among the guests were some Pharisees, unhappy with having to mingle with persons they considered ritually unclean. In what we call a stage whisper they muttered to the nearest disciple, "why does He associate with such disreputable persons, even eating with them?"

Hearing this, as He was meant to, Jesus replied:

"I've come as a physician to heal the sick. Those who are well have no need of a physician."

Levi had another name, Matthew, but we never used it after the election of Matthias to the "Twelve." You remember? After the Resurrection of Jesus Peter gathered the Apostles and asked them to elect someone to take the place of Judas the betrayer. It was thought fitting to preserve the sacred number "twelve." Matthias was chosen from the disciples who'd been with Jesus from the beginning of His ministry.

The two names sounded too similar! There were two disciples named "James," and two named "Judas," but we were used to that for three years. I think it was Matthew himself who preferred to use the name "Levi." This reminds me of Judas the Zealot who wished to be called Thaddeus after the defection of Judas Iscariot. His brother Simon, not Simon Peter, was also one of the Twelve.

Thomas was one of the well known disciples. He and I were not close, for I was uncomfortable with his examining mind. He needed to analyze and prove everything for himself. He always had some question, no matter what the subject. Doubt was part of him!

You see I knew some of the Twelve very well. Others were not as close to me. These are the names of the Twelve chosen by Jesus to be the foundation of a people of God renewed:

Peter, Andrew, James, John, Philip, Bartholomew (Nathaniel), Levi (Matthew), Thomas, James, Simon, Judas (Thaddeus) and Judas Iscariot (who betrayed Jesus).

Other Disciples

Besides the Twelve, other men and women became His disciples. Jesus trained a group of seventy, and He sent them out to prepare the way for His coming. Whereas the Twelve were sent out as sharers of His mission, the Seventy prepared for His mission. Only after His death was the mission of Jesus given to a larger group to share.

In sending out His missionaries, Jesus told them to travel light, to focus on the mission itself. They were to show their own trust in God's care when they proclaimed the Kingdom. If they were rejected, they were not to worry; they had done what they could. They were to shake the dust of such a place from their sandals. This is an ancient custom of our people, to shake the dust from our sandals when leaving a land of unbelievers.

Many women gladly heard Jesus' words and formed a group that cared for His practical needs. Mary Magdalene became their leader. In those times, as well as ours, women were not allowed to preach or teach in the synagogue. From the early days of our community, however, they have played an important role among us.

There were also secret disciples of Jesus. Among them were Joseph of Arimathea and Nicodemus, both members of the Sanhedrin, the Great Council that served as governing body of our people. It was presided over by the high priest and had what power the Romans allowed the Jews to have. Joseph and Nicodemus kept their places in the Sanhedrin but followed Jesus. This way they could inform Him of discussions and also put in a good word on His behalf.

I knew them slightly, as our families moved in the same social circles. I particularly remember what I heard of the night Nicodemus came to see Jesus:

To Be Born Again

Nicodemus was learned in both rabbinic and Hellenistic traditions. Himself a leading teacher in Jerusalem, he came to the Teacher whose fame had spread through the city that was the center of our Jewish traditions and belief. The miracles Jesus worked were signs of a power from above. Jesus listened to the learned man and commented:

"No one can enter the Kingdom of God unless he be born from above."

"Can I be born again? Can I enter my mother's womb and be born once more?"

"Physically, you are born of human parents. Spiritually, you are born of the Spirit."

Nicodemus became a disciple, but, as I've said, covertly. He continued to visit Jesus by night. This was a popular time for study with a rabbi, but it was also a time when few were abroad. He was less likely to be seen and reported to the Sanhedrin.

The Rich Young Man's Story

I too became a disciple. This is my story:

Jesus' sublime sermon on the Mount still rang in my ears. He had urged us to seek the life of the Kingdom. One day, I finally went up to Him. I asked:

"Teacher, what must I do to have eternal life?"

He looked into my eyes, and I felt His love. I know why so many leave everything to follow Him. In spite of this, I was unwilling to do so at this time. I heard His answer:

"Obey the commandments: do not murder, do not commit adultery, do not bear false witness, do not cheat, honor your father and your mother."

I told Jesus:

"I've kept these. What more must I do?"

"Go and sell all your have and give it to the poor. Then, come and follow Me."

I could not. I was so wealthy I was often called, "the rich young man." There were certain things I felt necessary for my comfort and security. Looking away, I backed off, ashamed. I felt His eyes following me and heard Him say:

"How hard it is for the rich to enter the Kingdom! It's easier for a camel to pass through the eye of a needle!"

Someone asked:

"Then who can be saved?"

Before I tell you Jesus' answer, let me remind you what a shock Jesus' idea was to everyone! Even today, and among our Christian people, there are some who consider material wealth a blessing from God, a sign of His favor. The poor are not favored. This was a powerful sentiment at the time, despite a contrary tradition of our people that proclaims God's particular love for the poor, so intense that among other sayings of our Scriptures is this: when you are kind to the poor you are lending to God, and God himself will repay you.

Now back to Jesus' answer to the despairing remark as to who can be saved?:

"For men and women, some things are impossible. For God, nothing is."

My story has a happy ending, as you can see! After all these years, I still hear His voice and feel His gaze. Gradually, I did become His disciple and His friend. He was the best of friends."

What did Jesus look like?

I asked the elder what Jesus looked like. He answered:

"I can hear His voice, but I cannot clearly see His face. The main reason is that I remember His appearance after He had risen from the dead. His body was the same body but glorified. One other reason is the great beauty of soul that shone on His face, even before His death and glorification.

The physical features of His face were secondary.

I do remember He was kind and gentle but quite virile and courageous. He was strong and healthy. Years of work with wood and blocks of stone had made Him hardy. This enabled Him to walk the length and breadth of the Land. He was a radiant light for our people. If I were asked what was the most characteristic of Jesus' personality I would say it was His kindness; He was kind, indeed."

The Talents

Speaking of kindness, to be kind is a sign that those in believe in Him are truly disciples, His followers. I have often repeated one of His parables that at first seems harsh, but Jesus wanted to stress the importance of putting our talents to use. Remember again that a parable has one main point, so that you should not try to understand and explain every detail. This is what Jesus said:

"A man about to go on a journey called his servants together to arrange for them to manage his property till he should return, and he gave each one a large sum of money. He gave one 5,000 talents, an enormous sum, indeed. To another 2,000 talents, also a huge sum. To a third he gave 1,000. The servants who had received 5,000 and 2,000 talents went out and invested the amount.

The third servant went and dug a hole in the ground and buried the 1,000 talents.

After a considerable time the owner of the property returned and called his servants to account for what they had done with the property in his absence. The first man said that he had invested the money entrusted to him and had earned an equal amount, handing his master the 10,000 talents.

The second man had done the same, investing and doubling his 2,000 talents. The third man told him how he had feared him and had hidden his 1,000 talents, keeping it safe but unused.

The man was pleased with the first two and commended them. The third man he reprimanded and took back his money with the comment, " take his money and give it to the others. To those who have more will be given. From those who have nothing even that will be taken away. Take that man and throw him outside in the darkness, where there will weeping and wailing and grinding of teeth"

I interrupted the old disciple to say:

"That sounds cruel to me, especially the last part. What does that mean? It doesn't sound sensible to me."

He patiently explained:

"That's because Jesus used an ancient proverb, one used to illustrate various parables and maxims.

Some of the very ancient proverbs are so Semitic, from a mind set different from what you too, in spite of your Semitic ancestry, are accustomed to in the West, that they are often not easily understood by non-Semitic people. The meaning is that those who use their gifts increase these gifts, to their own and to others' advantage. We must use our gifts, or they become rusty and useless to everyone, including ourselves, that is, not to use is the same as not to have.

Concerning the rejection of the fearful man into the darkness. It was his decision; he did not desire to be with his master, so it was his choice to be in the darkness. We all await our Master's return, when He will take us to our Father's home. Our God is a kindly God whose mercy is beyond our imagining, but we have to trust in Him. That gives us courage to use our talents.

We have different talents. Some are called to be leaders, because of their administrative gifts. Some are artists, painter or poets or musicians or storytellers. Some are builders and carpenters. Some are teachers. Some have less talents, but we all have the most important one, and we can all use this. We can all be kind!

SIGNS OF HIS GLORY

Jesus' mother often spoke of the wedding, at Cana, a village not far from Nazareth. I was not there, but it almost seems as if I were. At this feast Jesus worked His first miracle:

A gentle breeze cooled the already warm weather. The guests were happy. The bride and groom were poor, but the feast was grand, for they had spent all they had to make it an occasion of joy. Mary was there, with Jesus and some of His disciples. Now she was getting worried, as she whispered to her Son:

"They've run out of wine."

That's all Mary said to Jesus. She knew He would help. He was always a channel of joy. What is more joyful than a wedding? Nevertheless, He said, in a low voice:

"What has that to do with you and Me? My hour has not yet come."

Mary knew what He meant, that in spite of the mission for which the Spirit had come upon Him at His baptism and in spite of the signs of His extraordinary gifts of preaching He did not feel that God had yet endowed Him with the power to show why He had been chosen. In this hour it was Mary who was inspired. The Spirit spoke to her before her Son! With a mother's confidence in her Son, she beckoned to the servants. She advised them:

"Do whatever He tells you."

Jesus now realized His Father was using His mother's faith as the means of letting Him know His hour had come.

He had them fill the huge jars with water. Then, He told them to draw some out and take it to the chief steward. When the steward tasted it, he was pleased and surprised. He went to the bridegroom and said:

"Most people serve the best wine first. You've saved the best wine till now!"

One of the disciples there heard the remark, and it remained in his mind. One day, he saw a deeper meaning to the steward's observation. It was while he was at prayer in the Temple. At the start of a new moon we would sing the psalm praising God's work of creation:

"Bless the Lord, my soul.
O Lord,my God, how great You are!
You clothe Yourself with light.
You stretch the skies like a curtain...
You established the earth on its foundation...
You give drink to all the animals...
You cause the grass to grow...
You made wine to cheer the human heart...."

Everything was done to make us happy. A lovely old tradition of our people compares God's guiding word, His torah, to wine. Both give joy to the one who drinks it. God's final word, His Son, was among us.

Another tradition of old Israel compares her relation to God to that of a marriage. In His Son, God had come to this wedding. According to custom, the bridegroom provided wine for the feast. At Cana, the divine Bridegroom provided the best wine!

In His Son, God once again visited His people. This visit of God in His Son reminds me of another visit God made to His people, Adam and Eve, in the garden of Eden at the dawn of human history. We do not know details of creation, but the Spirit of God helped gifted forebears to tell the story that conveys the truth that God created the human race, and that somehow man, both male and female, have a tendency to turn away from God and do their own will instead of His. The scene was laid out for us in the book of Genesis:

God was walking in the garden He made for Adam and Eve and gave them to tend. He was taking the soft summer breeze that blows in from the sea. Something was wrong. Adam and Eve always ran out, carefree and happy, to meet Him. This evening, they were not there.

God's creative hand had formed Adam and Eve as a potter forms vessels of clay. Taking earth, He made a physical form, a body. Then He breathed life into the body, and it became a human person, body and soul.

The crown of creation is man, male and female, made in God's own image and likeness and given life by His divine breath.

For their home, God gave Adam and Eve an earthly paradise, the garden of Eden. They could eat the fruit of any tree, with one exception. They were not to even touch the deadly fruit of the tree of knowing good and evil.

While God was absent, Satan, prince of evil spirits, appeared. Driven by envy of human happiness, the devil entered the garden, where he had no right to be. He had taken the body of a serpent, a beast considered of old to be the cleverest and most deceptive of non-human creatures.

You know that a spirit can take a body for a limited time. A spirit cannot change, however. Unholy spirits chose, once and for all, to disobey God. Holy spirits, our angels, obey God and guide us.

All spirits see something of God in Adam and Eve, and their children. Because of this devils hate us. The prince of devils enticed the child-like Eve. He uttered the first lie heard on the face of the earth:

"Why did God forbid you to eat this fruit? He's afraid you'll become like Him, knowing good and evil."

Naive and inexperienced, Eve yielded to temptation. She ate the forbidden fruit and found it agreeable. She gave some to Adam, and he ate. Their innocence was gone. Now they knew both good and evil and hid themselves in shame.

God called them and told them they had to leave their earthly paradise. It was not the end, however. He had a plan, which we now know; He would send His own divine Son to share our human life and so represent us all in doing God's will and undoing the mistake of Adam and Eve.

The Son of God became a man, in our Hebrew tongue this means a son of man. "Son of Man" can also refer to a prophet, one who speaks for God. Jesus of course filled both functions, representing both God and the whole human race, speaking for God and speaking for us! He would obey His Father's voice and thus undo the harm done by the disobedience of Adam and Eve. For everyone who follows His way, the way of love, the gate to a new paradise would be opened. The new paradise, the kingdom of God, is far more wonderful than the one lost, because that was a merely earthly one.

God can bring good out of evil. He has in mind for each of us a wondrous gift, a share in His own life!

The water made wine was the first manifestation of God's glory in His Son. Where God is, there is His glory. As Son of God, Jesus is divine and always has this glory. As Son of Man, that is human, Jesus received it when His hour had come.

Jesus, Son of God and Son of Man. Divine and at the same time fully human, learning by experience as we all do. The union of the human and the divine in Jesus is beyond the limits of our human reasoning. Faith reaches beyond these limits, and Mary lived by faith.

Every day was not a Cana for Mary! Her faith in her Son was sometimes tested. Smiling at the memory, she told of the time she had feared for her

Son's safety and tried to get Him to take a break in His impassioned teaching. I'll tell you what I remember of Mary's account of that day:

Mary was at home when one of the disciples ran in, breathless and agitated. He said the crowd listening to Jesus had turned angry and threatening. Mary called the rest of the family and hurried with them to the place where Jesus was speaking.

Told His mother and brothers were outside and wanted to see Him, Jesus looked around and said:

"Who is My mother, My brothers, My sisters? Whoever does the will of My Father is brother, sister, mother to Me."

Jesus was not denigrating His much loved mother but teaching that faith in Him is a stronger bond than that of blood. Mary's faith in Him was a spiritual relationship, deeper than the physical relationship established by giving Him birth. She believed in Him, as He believed in His Father. Jesus too lived by faith!

Jesus at Capharnaum

Among the lovely little towns of Galilee, Jesus' favorite was Capharnaum, on the shore of the sea of Galilee. Galilee is a most pleasant area, fertile and green, and the great lake gives an aura of peace to everything close by. The location of this "village of Nahum" on the important road between Egypt and Damascus made it friendly and welcoming. It soon became the center of Jesus' Galilean ministry, where He spent most of His time, going up to Jerusalem a few times a year, on the occasion of the great pilgrimage feasts.

I had a house there, where I spent time during the winter, as the shore of the lake is quite warm in the summer. Peter also had a house there; he had moved there from his original home at Bethsaida , a village also on the lake. Capharnaum was a more flourishing center for fishing, and Peter's wife was living there with her mother. Peter helped Jesus obtain a large house close to the lake shore and not far at all from the synagogue. Jesus brought Mary and other members of the family there, besides a few disciples.

Peter's description of what happened one Sabbath day was so vivid that even now I seem to have witnessed it myself:

On this Sabbath morning Jesus was about to leave for the synagogue, which was newly built and quite close to His house, stone's throw from the lake itself. Peter arrived to tell Him his mother-in-law was ill with fever.

Jesus assured him all would be well; He'd go to see her after the morning prayer. They went together to the place of prayer and study.

Jesus was invited to read and comment on the sacred text. As He did, the congregation was appreciative, and amazed. It was not just the beauty of His voice or His convincing manner. What astounded them was the authority with which He spoke.

This was something new. All our rabbis and scribes spoke on the authority of someone else. They would cite a well known teacher of Torah as authority for their own opinions. When they taught, they would bolster their teaching by saying, "as Rabbi so and so says."

Jesus was His own authority. When He taught, He simply said: I tell you....

On this Sabbath day, His authority was challenged even before He left the synagogue. The challenge was not from those who had heard His teaching but from an intruder; a man possessed by an unclean spirit came in as Jesus was about to leave.

Let me interrupt my own narrative for a minute here to tell you of our tradition concerning unclean or unholy spirits. Satan and his host of evil and unholy spirits frequent places that are unclean and relate in some way to death, such as the lifeless desert, and tombs, and refuse dumps. Such a filthy place used to be here -look over there, to the left. See the valley we call Hinnom or Gehenna in Greek. It is now, as you see, green covered with great rocky masses sticking out here and there. In the time of Jesus it was still the main refuse dump for Jerusalem, and fires burned there without ceasing, day and night.. It became for us a symbol of hell, home of the unholy.

Back to the synagogue in Capharnaum. With the superior sight of a spirit, the unholy creature saw in Jesus the One who would destroy its power. Defiantly, the evil spirit called out:

"What do You want with us, Jesus of Nazareth? Are You here to destroy us? I know who You are, God's Holy One."

To know one's name is to enjoy some power over that person. Jesus showed that evil has no power over Him. He said:

"Be quiet. Come out of him."

The evil spirit departed.

Having freed the man of the diabolical possession, Jesus continued on His way to Peter's home. He took the sick woman by the hand and healed her. Within minutes, she was bustling about to prepare the food she then served them herself!

At sunset, as the Sabbath ended, many came from neighboring places to experience Jesus' healing touch. News of the expulsion of the unclean spirit had traveled fast, in spite of the sabbath! Meeting their faith, Jesus healed them of their ills. They left in peace.

The Storm on the Lake

Jesus was now exhausted. He asked some disciples to row Him to the other shore of the lake. Several boats set out together. It was dark, but the waters of the lake were at rest. Jesus fell asleep in the boat.

Sleep. In our Hebrew tradition a symbol of faith and trust in the Lord's care for us. David the King once sang of his own trust that the Lord watched over him as he slept. Do you remember the verse?

"I will lie down in peace, and sleep comes at once, for You alone, Lord, make me dwell secure."

With His pure heart, unencumbered and trusting, Jesus was sleeping. He was not naive. He knew what lay ahead. What allowed Him to sleep so soundly was His trust in His Father, and He wanted His disciples to share His faith.

Without warning, a storm burst upon the lake. It whipped the waves in its rage, tossing the boat up and down, as if to sink it. The disciples were used to sudden storms, but this was worse than usual. One of them, perhaps Peter himself, yelled to Jesus:

"Don't You care if we drown?!"

With the same simple command He had given earlier that day to the demon, Jesus spoke to the raging wind:

"Be quiet. Be still."

The wind obeyed, and a great calm came upon the sea. Jesus' own peace was felt in the still of the night. The stars appeared above, and the water now gently lapped against the wood of the boat. For the second time that day, the question was posed:

"What kind of man is He?"

Remember. Ancient traditions see unruly nature as demonic powers personified. Uncontrolled winds seem to defy the ordering of nature, as if in ongoing revolt against the Creator. God is, however, master of all these powers. To command the wind, to calm the raging sea, this is a sign of His presence. This was one more sign of Jesus' power.

Peter urged me to engrave this scene on my memory, as he had. It had helped him through many storms in his own soul. In times of fear or distress or doubt, he would stop and listen for Jesus' voice:

"Be quiet. Be still."

The Lilies of the Field

We sat around Jesus on the ground at the shore of the lake, not far from Capharnaum, a smaller group than usual, as it was somewhat early in the morning. The weather was just about perfect, after the latter rains of late winter. The air was fresh and mild with a light breeze blowing, and the grass was still thick and dotted with bright colored flowers we collectively called lilies of the field.

Peter had told me He was going to ask Jesus to address the problem I shared with many others, that is, trying to serve two masters, money and God! Money of course is not just the gold and silver but anything of a world that is in fact passing.

He laid open the heart of the matter: can we be in fact as independent as our focus on money and other means of security would seem to imply? Does not life itself tell us that we are dependent? He reminded us that all the anxiety in the world cannot add an inch to our height or a day to our life!

He drew attention to the beauty of the lilies of the field all around us and to the cheerful twitter of the birds as they hopped and flew about in their search of food ready at hand. He said that we should draw a lesson from the flowers and the birds, all taken care of by the same God who cares for us and who loves us infinitely more than them! He did not tell us not to worry at all but not to be overcome by anxiety, a state of mind that can choke the hope in our hearts.

The secret was given to us as He urged us to seek first the kingdom of God, that is, what is eternal and unending happiness. When we do that it is so much easier to fit everything in, all the trials and sorrows and pain that are a part of our lives here on earth. He advised us to live day by day,

"Don't worry so much about tomorrow; today has enough troubles of its own!"

THE OUTSIDER

The Passover was a few days away, and I was in Jerusalem for the feast. Hearing that Jesus was visiting His friends in Bethany, I walked up to meet Him. I found Him here, at this very spot, teaching. It was a favorite place. On rainy days the grotto behind us offered shelter; at all times, we could look across the valley to the City and its Temple.

That morning we looked at a Temple in all its glory, despite the clouds that hid the sun. After all these years, I still remember that dreary day. The cheerless sky was a fit setting for Jesus' prophetic lament:

"The day will come when this Temple we're admiring will be destroyed. Not a stone will stand upon a stone."

Stunned and silent, we got up and walked with Him on His way down the mountain. After only a few paces, He stopped and gazed at the Holy City. It was beautiful to behold, fine weather or foul. Look at it even now, with its many ruins. Try to imagine its beauty as Jesus saw it.

Jesus began to weep. This was rare for Him, and it confused us. Looking back, I realize now that He was near the end of His strength. He had worked so hard to bring the good news to the people He loved, His own people. To see them slip away was a bitter cup to drink. He spoke in prophecy:

"Jerusalem, Jerusalem. To be ruined because you did not recognize the Lord when He came to visit you."

To many of His own people, Jesus was an outsider. Mystery indeed: born outside Bethlehem, He was to die outside Jerusalem. Even Nazareth rejected one of its own. He became an outsider to the very place where He had grown to manhood. Early in His ministry He left Nazareth forever. Let me tell you what I myself saw, to my sorrow.

Nazareth has changed a little since Jesus' time, but it's still a charming, out-of-the-way place. Not long after my first encounter with Jesus at Capharnaum, I went up to Nazareth to hear Him speak. Already, I could not miss and opportunity to hear Him, for when He spoke, it was as if He had been sent to answer the questions I had concerning my life, where was I going, and life itself, what is it all about?

Jesus returned to His hometown a famous Man. I was at first surprised to see how little He was esteemed in the very place where I expected Him to an object of local pride. He was honored and respected in every place but Nazareth!

On the Sabbath we went to the synagogue. Outside, a few sick had come to be healed. As it turned out, they were the only ones to believe in Him. He laid His hands on them and made them well. Inside, Inside, the leader of the synagogue invited Him to read and comment on the sacred text.

It was from the book of Isaiah the prophet. You recall: the Prophet cries out that the spirit of the Lord has come upon him, to proclaim good news to the poor, freedom for prisoners, sight for the blind, and to announce that the time has come when the Lord will save His people. Jesus then rolled up the scroll and sat down to speak.

Their eyes were fixed on Him. He had never spoken before in His own synagogue . It was the custom, of course, for the leader of the synagogue to invite different members to read and then comment on the sacred text. At least the leader, if the only one among the Nazarenes, knew of Jesus' reputation as a healer and a preacher. What would He say?

He said: "Today, as these words echo in your ears, the prophecy is being fulfilled."

In a beautiful and moving homily He developed this thought, enlarging upon God's plan to save His people. At first, there were murmurs of approval and appreciation, but then they began to nudge one another and exchange negative looks. While He was still speaking they muttered to each other, loud enough for Jesus to hear:

"Where'd He get all this wisdom? He's no smarter than we are. He was an ordinary worker like the rest of us. His mother and His family are still here. They're nothing special, either."

Jesus was taken aback by their lack of faith. Well liked all His life, He had grown up with these people. Many of them had tables and chairs and even houses He had built. They had seemed to be His friends and appreciate His ideas. He had to remark:

"A prophet is not without honor except in His own land."

They stood up. They would hear no more. They even threatened Him, so Jesus left their synagogue for good, stopping on the way to lay His hands on a few sick men and women who had come during His sermon to receive healing as He left. The men followed Him as He departed , even yelling that they would throw Him off the brow of the hill at the edge of town.

This was bluster only, for they were few were well aware that Jesus was a gentle person but very strong, and who knew whether He would defend Himself and in the struggle perhaps one or more of them would go down the steep hillside for a most uncomfortable distance? In the event, Jesus ignored them and turned towards the East to go down the road towards the more hospitable Capharnaum that lay by the shore of the sea of Galilee.

I should point out that Jesus' sorrow at this rejection by His own villagers was not primarily a personal hurt. Of course, He was deeply affected, for He was sensitive and wanted His love to be reciprocated. Still, what most grieved Him was that He knew what these indifferent and hostile people were missing. This is why He wept over Jerusalem later on.

Experiencing what it means to be an outsider, Jesus was all the more eager to reach out to anyone finding himself or herself in this unwelcome state. He offered love to the unloved and the poor, and the lonely, the shunned, and to all of low self esteem. He spoke to them of a Father's care and concern for them. I myself witnessed several such encounters.

The Man in the Sycamore Tree

Two of them occured in Jericho. Go down yourself and see this city of palms. It lies in the Jordan valley, a land that bakes in the sun, to the north of the lake without life. Jericho itself is an oasis in this low-lying land; a spring of living water keeps its orchards and groves green and fruitful.

In the days of Joshua, Jericho heard the sound of Israel's trumpets, and her walls came tumbling down. You know that "Joshua" and "Jesus" are forms of the same name that means "God saves." Joshua's saving deeds were a distant foreshadowing of the salvation Jesus was to bring one day to Jericho:

I was there that day, sitting with Zacchaeus in the shade of an old sycamore tree. I had just settled the taxes on the orange groves I had near Jericho. The day was typical of Jericho most of the time, very hot, with no movement of air. We were sipping mint flavored tea to keep cool.

Zacchaeus was an outsider. He was Jewish, but a tax collector. To be a tax collector was to be an outsider, at least to some of our people. Many tax collectors were in fact dishonest. All of them, in some way, served Rome, the non-Jewish master of our land.

Zacchaeus, however, was honest, and he lived the Law in his daily life. He was well named, Zakkai, that is,"pure of heart." He used the Greek form of this name, Zacchaeus, for business. When he heard Jesus was coming, he jumped up, knocking over his tea! The whole city was just as excited, and the street was soon thronged.

Zacchaeus was short, and taller men already crowded the edge of the road. True to his simple approach to everything, he climbed the sycamore to get a better view! He was well known locally, and I could hear voices commenting on his handling of the situation. Jesus heard them, too, and called to the man He recognized as a kindred spirit:

"Zacchaeus, come down. I'm going to eat at your house today."

He was overcome, grateful and happy, and he made his way through the crowd to the Healer of souls. The murmuring began:

"Is this Man going to the house of a sinner?"

The people of Jericho were in no position to point out the faults of anyone else. Instead of saying so, Zacchaeus told Jesus he would give half of all he had to the poor. Furthermore, if it could be shown that by chance he had cheated anyone, he would repay the victim fourfold.

Jesus replied, for all to hear:

"Salvation has come this day to this man's house. He too is a son of Abraham, and the Son of man has come to search for the lost and save them."

The Blind Beggar

Jesus' second saving deed that day in Jericho actually was done a little while before this. What I'm telling you now I heard from the man himself, Bartimaeus. He too wanted to see, and he too had to rise above discouraging words.

As Jesus approached the city, the poorer folk gathered outside. They were eager to greet Him, this kind man from Galilee. Many in Jericho considered Him to be the Messiah himself. Among these poor folk was Bartimaeus, at the side of the road, blind and a beggar.

Poverty had caused Bartimaeus to lose his sight as a child. Poor vision or even blindness is common among the poor in dry regions, due to the dust. Unable to work, Bartimaeus had to beg for food and clothing. He had nothing but his hope.

This day his hope served him well. When he heard the commotion, he asked what was happening.

"It's Jesus of Nazareth."

He had heard of Him, the teacher whose healing power gave the poor and the simple folk the hope that He was the longed for Messiah, the son of David. As he struggled to his feet, Bartimaeus called out:

"Son of David, help me!"

Jesus heard him. Seeing he was blind, He asked disciples to go and bring the man to Him. He asked him:

"What do you want Me to do for you?"

"I want to see."

Freeing him from his blindness, the Savior said:

"Go in peace. Your faith has saved you."

After years of blindness, Bartimaeus saw again, and he He followed Jesus on His way.

The Lonely Leper

"Lord, if You want to, You can heal me."

I still hear that voice, of a leper, on his knees before Jesus. He had been waiting outside the little village, on the dry and dusty path He knew Jesus would use. A young man, he was shunned and avoided, and he was very lonely. Only death looked his way, and it was grinning.

This time, death gloated too soon. When I speak of death, it's not just the absence of physical life. In the ancient tradition of our Jewish forebears death is also and above all the absence of friends and associates in this life. This young man should have been with other young people. Although the lower part of his face was terribly disfigured, one could see a well formed head and body. According to the Law, he had to be isolated.

Old laws of our people declared lepers unclean, that is, unholy. Lest they contaminate the purity, the holiness as they saw it, of the community, they were to be kept outside the camp. Practically, of course, this guarded against contagion. For the leper, it was a form of death.

To most people, the sight of this youth was unpleasant. To Jesus it was a plea for help. He asked him:

"What can I do to help you?"

"Lord," he said, "if You want to, You can make me clean."

Jesus assured him:

"I do want to."

He healed the grateful youth, restoring him to the life of the community.

A Centurion's Faith

Jesus had been sent to the house of Israel. According to our tradition, Israel was chosen and set apart by God to preserve and to share the light of His revelation. Jesus limited His ministry to Israel and Samaria, the latter because He often passed that way. Faith, however, never failed to elicit His response. At least twice, He healed Gentiles, truly outsiders in the minds of most Jews.

I was witness to one of these. Jesus was coming to take up residence at Capharnaum. He had just been expelled from His home town of Nazareth. A Gentile's faith was balm to soothe Him.

As we neared the town, we were met by a delegation of its citizens. They were accompanying the Roman centurion, whose servant was seriously ill. He was well known as a benefactor to our people. Their synagogue had just been completed with great help from this Gentile.

Knowing Jesus' general rule to minister only to His own people, the Jewish leaders came to ask Him to help this righteous Gentile. He readily agreed to go to the officer's house and heal his servant. The centurion replied:

"Lord, I am not worthy that You should enter under my roof. Say but the word, and my servant will be healed. I too am a man of authority. I say to one: do this, and he does it. If You say my servant will be healed, I know he will be healed."

Jesus was astounded and delighted. This faith in Him on the lips of a Gentile came at just the right time. He still felt the pain and humiliation of His rejection at Nazareth. He turned to us and said:

"I've not found such faith in Israel!"

He said to the centurion:

"Go home now, and you'll find what you've believe I can do has been done."

The Persistent Gentile Mother

Peter told me of another occasion when Jesus healed a non-Jewish person:

It was one of Jesus' rare excursions outside the land of Israel. He had gone to the region of the great city of Tyre, in neighboring Phoenicia. In those days there were more Jews there, but it was a Gentile city. Jesus needed a respite from the growing hostility of His own people.

He wanted a rest, but He'd become known to the local merchants in their business trips to Galilee. Hearing He was near, a woman came to ask His help. Her daughter was possessed by a demon. Would He free her?

More for the benefit of His Jewish disciples than for this Gentile woman, Jesus told her:

"It's not right to give the children's food to the dogs."

She knew of His troubles among His own people, and her reply revived Jesus' spirit:

"Even the dogs eat the scraps the children throw on the ground."

Pleased with her dogged faith, Jesus said:

"Your faith is refreshing. Go in peace. You'll find your daughter freed from the demon's grip."

Jesus and the Samaritans

Of all outsiders shunned by Jews, the most detested were the Samaritans. Once, a heckler could think of no greater insult to hurl at Jesus than:

"You're crazy. Besides, You're a Samaritan!"

Almost alone among His fellow Jews, Jesus reached out to the Samaritans. Jews and Samaritans were both children of Abraham, and of Jacob (remember: Jacob is the other name for Israel, for whom our people were named). Both Jew and Samaritan revered Moses as mediator of God's Torah to them. Yet, a mutual hostility separated them. You know the cause?

Remember the Babylonian captivity? Many centuries ago the northern and southern kingdoms of our people were conquered by the Assyrians and the Babylonians. The leader types were all deported to the lands of their conquerors. The humble folk were left to tend the land.

The Hebrew people deported to Assyria were assimilated there. Those deported to Babylon, the Hebrew princes, priests, and scholars managed to consolidate their traditions and even emerge as a more united society while in exile. After seventy years of this exile, they were allowed to return to their land. There, they found the poor folk had mingled and married with Gentile colonists sent in by the conquerors.

These simple folk had preserved their faith and kept the Five Books of the law of Moses as their guide, their Torah. In spite of this, the returning Jews, the people of Judah, looked askance at these humble folk. They treated them as outsiders and would not allow them to help rebuild Jerusalem and its temple. They were kept outside the Holy City.

Spurned and rejected, these simple children of Abraham and Jacob set up their own temple on Mount Gerizim, in the land of Samaria. This hilly land stretches between Galilee and Judah, or Judea, as we now say. The mountain itself overlooks the city and fields of Shechem, where our Fathers Abraham,Isaac, and Jacob once pastured their flocks.

Gerizim was a holy mountain long before the Samaritans raised their temple on its height. At its foot, Joshua had assembled the Israelites after their entry into the Promised Land. There they promised fidelity to the Lord. In the days of Joseph and his brothers, our father Jacob dug a well not far from Shechem. It's still there, its water cold and delicious.

The Woman at the Well

One day, Jesus sat by this well, tired and thirsty. The weather was warm, waiting for the cooling rain of the fall. The noonday sun had forced Him to stop and rest in the shade. While we went to the town for provisions, Jesus stayed by the well. A woman of the town appeared, with a water jar.

The woman at the well. Her encounter with Christ shows how faith in Him can come about. She told us of their talk together. Jesus asked her for a drink of water. Perceiving Him to be a Jew, she asked how it was that He would ask her, a Samaritan, for a drink of water. His answer was mystifying:

"If you recognized God's gift, that is, Who's asking you for a drink of water, you'd ask Him to give you a drink, and He'd give you a drink of the water of life."

This was a way Jesus led people to the truth. Usually, He told a parable to attract and help the hearer to remember. At other times, He spoke more directly, on a deeper level, as He did here.

This was the case when He discerned intellectual gifts in the hearer. He read the mind of the Samaritan woman and saw she was seeking something more than her life was providing.

For her part, the woman also recognized that Jesus was a cut above the ordinary. Following His lead, she said:

"This well is deep, and You have no bucket. Or are You more powerful than our father Jacob?"

Drawing her on to the truth, Jesus asked her to go and get her husband. She said she had none. Jesus told her:

"That's right. You've had five, and the man with whom you're now living is not your husband!"

Amazed, and ashamed, she turned the subject to religion:

"You are a prophet, I see. We worship God on this holy mountain, but you Jews say Jerusalem is the place where He should be worshiped.

Then, Jesus prophesied:

"The time is coming when you will worship the Father neither here nor in Jerusalem, but in spirit and in truth."

This prophecy was beyond her understanding at the time, but it was one she could not forget. She became herself a follower of Jesus. Her conversion was almost instant. She thought:

"He must be our Tabeh, the One who is to come, the One the Jews call the Messiah. Who else could discern the depths of my heart? There's nothing He doesn't know about me, and yet, He accepts me. I'll be His disciple."

She asked us if we would wait while she hurried to the town to bring others to meet Him.

Samaritans were not always so hospitable! Although Jesus was so friendly to them that other Jews could mockingly call Him a Samaritan, I still recall the time, only some days before this meeting, when a Samaritan town refused to receive Him. We had just crossed into Samaria, on our way up to the Holy City. The very sight of Jews on their way to Jerusalem annoyed the Samaritans.

As we neared the town, Jesus sent James and John on ahead to see if He would be received. The two brothers came back in a black mood; they had not been received. They suggested calling down fire from heaven to destroy the inhospitable town, but Jesus had to remind them this was not His way....

On this same journey from Galilee to Jerusalem, a single Samaritan showed more regard for Jesus than His own countrymen. Two or three days before our experiencing the unreceptive attitude of that Samaritan town we met ten lepers outside a village in the border area of Galilee and Samaria. From a distance they called to Him:

"Jesus, Master, help us!"

Jesus went over to them and asked where they were from. Nine were Jewish. The tenth was a Samaritan. Jesus blessed them and told them to go and show themselves to a priest, to be certified as clean and able to resume community life. They went, believing His word.

As they were on their way, they saw their skin return to normal. One of them ran back to thank the Healer. Jesus was disappointed that only one had come back to thank Him. This man was the Samaritan.

The Good Samaritan

"If you obey My commands, you will be My people, and I will be your God."

The Lord said this when he gave a covenant to our forebears. The condition laid down for Israel to be His people was their fulfillment of His commands.

Jesus gave an example of a man who fulfilled the conditions of the covenant between God and His people. He was a Samaritan!

The Samaritan's good deed was narrated by Jesus in response to a question posed by a teacher of Torah. Since Jesus was not known to have studied with a reputable rabbi, the scribe thought He would be shaky and vulnerable in any rabbinic discussion of Torah. To trap Him, the lawyer asked His opinion on a popular question among scholars:

"Master, what must I do to have eternal life?"

Ignoring the ill will He recognized, Jesus answered:

"What does it say in the Law?"

"You shall love the Lord your God with your whole heart and soul and mind, with all your strength, and your neighbor as yourself."

Jesus then suggested, "Do this, and you will live."

Sidestepping the suggestion, the lawyer posed a further question, one much debated at the time:

"And who is my neighbor?"

By way of answer, Jesus told this story:

"Robbers fell upon a man on the lonely road between Jerusalem and Jericho. Taking everything he had, they left him half dead by the side of the road. A priest came along. At the sight of the man lying there, he went to the other side of the road. Later, a levite came along. He too left the man lying by the side of the road.

The next man to come along was a Samaritan. Moved with pity, he did what he could for the man. He put him on his donkey and took him to the inn further along that road. He gave the sympathetic innkeeper money to care for him and promised to return and reimbourse him for anything else on his way back."

Jesus asked the teacher of Torah:

"Which of these was neighbor to the man in need?"

Chagrined, the lawyer replied:

"The one who helped him in his need."

Jesus concluded the conversation:

"Go and do the same."

PRAYER

A most extraordinary event occurred in the final months of Jesus' life here on earth. It was also most extraordinary for His closest friends, Peter, James, and John. It was so above the ordinary that theses three disciples were unable to grasp its full meaning until the Spirit came upon them after Jesus had risen from the dead. It was a mystical experience of Jesus at prayer.

All three disciples at some time spoke of this experience, for it was very important for Jesus and for them. It happened soon after Peter had received a revelation from God himself concerning Jesus' identity, that is, who He truly was and what He was to do. Before I recount this wondrous event in Jesus' life let me tell you of Peter's revelation.

This occurred at Caesarea Philippi or nearby, where the river Jordan begins to flow towards the south, through Galilee and along the borders of Samaria and Judea and then on into the Dead Sea.

This semi-pagan place was a bit remote from the main stream of Jewish life, and Jesus found it a place where He could rest from the now increasingly virulent attacks of His opponents.

I was there with Jesus as He waited for His disciples to return from the mission He had given them, that is, to spread the good news. Here too, my memory is not perfect, but as I recall, when they had gathered together He asked:

"Who do people say I am?"

"Some say John the Baptist, come back to life. Some say You're Elijah or Jeremiah, or another prophet."

"Who do you say I am?!"

Peter spoke in the Spirit:

"You are the Messiah, Son of the living God."

Jesus was very happy, for Peter's answer confirmed His choice of Peter as the man to shepherd His flock. The end of Jesus' earthly mission loomed ahead, and He had to provide for the little flock His death would leave behind. From the beginning Peter had been the spokesman for the group of disciples, enthusiastic at times and impetuous but always eager to learn from Jesus and ready to obey the prompting and direction of the Spirit.

Jesus now blessed him:

"Happy man, Simon, son of John! Only My Father could have told you this. Now I tell you. You are Peter, the rock on which I will build My church. Hell itself will never hold out against it! I will give you the keys of the Kingdom. Whatever you bind or loose on earth will be bound or loosed in heaven!"

At the time, this was mysterious to Peter, and to us. After Jesus rose from the dead and gave us His Spirit, then the blessing on Peter made sense. It was never forgotten, although not understood when spoken.

Jesus knew His man. Peter was loving and loyal, flexible and forgiving. Devoted to His teacher he was ever ready to speak and to act. He was humbly able to admit mistakes and get on with things. Peter's Teacher saw him as one through whom He could safely guide His flock to the gates of the Kingdom.

The Transfiguration

Now for the experience of Jesus at prayer. We had left the area of Caesarea Philippi. Before us rose a mighty mountain, a natural place to seek the face of God, that is, to pray. We did not ascend this time, for Jesus left the rest of His disciples and took His three favorite friends and disciples with Him. They started early in the morning, to get to the top of the high hill before the heat of day. As they neared the summit the sky was clear and cloudless.

The climax of Jesus' mission was coming closer, for His opponents now openly threatened His life, actually plotting in plain sight. It was time, Jesus knew, to leave Galilee for the less friendly Judea. By now Jesus also knew He would die there, in Jerusalem. So this bright summer's day He went up the mountain to be reassured, and He took the three pillars of His little community with Him, for their future confidence in days of darkness and doubt. He dreaded the coming test, and He knew His disciples would be shocked and demoralized. They all needed to hear the voice of the Father.

When they reached the top of the mountain, Jesus went off a little by Himself, to be alone with His Father, while the three disciples sat nearby to rest. Jesus of course prayed as He often told us we should pray, as children listening to the Father they know loves them and enjoys being with them, reassuring them.

As Jesus prayed, His friends dozed from fatigue but woke at the sudden shining of bright light.

Before their eyes Jesus was transfigured, flooded with divine light, His face shining as the sun, His clothes dazzlingly white. Moses, the lawgiver and Elijah, the prophet who had conversed with God in olden times, privileged to see His glory, now conversed with His Son, Jesus the Christ.

Peter, James, and John were overwhelmed, unable at the time to comprehend the mystery. It was too wonderful to forget, but at the moment they acted like the fishermen from Galilee they were.

Not really knowing what he was saying, Peter blurted out:

"Lord, let us build three shrines here, one for You, one for Moses, and one for Elijah."

The cloud of glory, sign of God's presence, appeared, and the voice of the Father was heard, the same voice once heard by Moses and later by Elijah at the same holy mountain that was called either Horeb or Sinai. Now God spoke to the three fishermen of Galilee:

"This is My beloved Son. Listen to Him."

God speaks from now on in His Son. Jesus it the full and perfect revelation of God. Everything God wants us to know about Himself can be known when we listen to the voice of His Son. When we listen to Christ we are listening to God.

Jesus wanted this vision of His glory to be kept secret until the proper time, for this would only confirm current notions of salvation as linked to external signs of power and might, even to force of arms, so He sternly told the three witnesses:

"Tell the vision to no one until I rise from the dead."

The disciples obeyed His order; they never mentioned the vision until Jesus had indeed risen from the dead. Then they understood its significance and the danger of conceiving Jesus' messianic role as political. Their faith was still weak; in spite of the fact that the disciples Jesus had sent out to preach and heal had returned with success stories as a group His disciples did not always manifest a confidence in the power He had given them. This was evident in an unhappy incident at the foot of the mountain where God's glory had been revealed in Jesus.

Once Moses had come down from the mountain top his face still glowing from his encounter with God's glory to find his disciples in a state of faithlessness (remember they had asked Aaron to make them a golden calf to worship). Now, Jesus came down from His experience of divine light and found His disciples without the faith they needed to heal a boy possessed of an evil spirit that had made the lad act as an epileptic. The boy's father came to Jesus and told Him that His disciples had been unable to drive out the evil spirit.

Jesus rarely showed any irritation, but at times He did. This was one of those times! He was annoyed at the weak faith the disciples showed in not driving out the evil spirit; He even exclaimed:

"Unbelieving people. How long must I be with you?!"

As He ordered the boy to be brought over to Him the boy's father begged him to help if He could. This upset Jesus even more! He again made reference to lack of faith, to which the desperate father humbly replied:

"Help my weak faith."

By way of response Jesus healed the boy. That prayer of the father, "help my weak faith," still sounds in my soul, after all these years. Sometimes, my own faith is weak, but Jesus never leaves unanswered that father's prayer for stronger faith. I often make that prayer my own!

The disciples naively asked Jesus why they had been unable to drive out the evil spirit, to which Jesus replied, using the hyperbole our Semitic people so love:

"Your faith is too weak. If you had faith the size of a tiny mustard seed you could tell a mountain to move, and it would!"

Peter insisted that he heard Jesus say that only prayer could drive out such an evil spirit. It's the same thing, namely, that when we pray for anything our faith has to be confident, that what we ask is granted by God. Sometimes He does not grant our exact wish, for He knows best what is good for us, but He always answers the prayer in the way He knows will most benefit us.

From this place He led us southwards, towards Jerusalem the Holy City. As we walked along, Jesus opened His heart to us:

"The Son of Man must suffer much from the scribes, the elders, and the chief priests. He will be rejected and put to death. On the third day He will rise to life."

Peter was incredulous; he had just seen the vision of glory descend from heaven upon the Son of Man, their Teacher. He said to Jesus:

"This will never happen to You, Lord."

In front of everyone, Jesus rebuked him:

"You speak like Satan, who tempts Me to avoid the suffering that leads to glory. I have to suffer. So do you, if you wish to follow Me. You have to take up your cross, as I will. A dry dead kernel of wheat has to fall to the ground in order to live again. To live, you have to die."

To Drink His Cup

Not long after this the mother of James and John brought her two sons to Jesus and asked Him the favor of their sitting at His right and left when He should come into His kingdom, that is, when glory would be His. Actually, it was the two themselves who did the requesting, for the glory they had seen on the mountain still burned in their souls. Since they were close to Him, why should they not be given such good places? They had not told anyone, including their mother, obedient to Jesus, but they obviously scarcely understood or accepted what Jesus had just said to Peter.

Jesus asked them if they could drink the cup He would drink. In their usual buoyant manner the two brothers said they could. To which Jesus said:

"From My cup you will drink, but it's not for Me to assign places in the Kingdom but rather for My Father."

When the others heard of this they began to reproach James and John for their presumption, but Jesus placed the whole question on a higher level, repeating once again the necessity to live on the level of the spiritual. Rulers of this age make their power felt, but the Son of Man came not to be served but to serve. Whoever aspires to be truly great must imitate Jesus, the greatest of all, who was to give His very life for others.

The prayer of the two brothers was heard, for we know that with God there is no distance from those He loves and who love Him in return. The places they now have are incomparably more wonderful, and glorious, than what they asked for!

Persevere in Prayer

Whenever He spoke of His Father Jesus' face glowed! He wanted us to experience this love. He said that we should remember how parents delight in making their children happy and secure. He asked us if we thought our heavenly Father is less loving than we are! He added that we should persevere in praying for what we need. To make His point He told a delightful story.

He pictured a man snug in bed who woke to a pounding at his door. Whoever was knocking would not stop, so he called out:

"Who's there?"

It was a neighbor whose friend had come, unexpected, and he had nothing to give him. Our man replied that he was in bed with his family and could not get up to help him, so he said:

"Go away."

The neighbor kept knocking until the man finally got up and gave him what he needed. Even though the man in bed was not intended to represent God, we did think of that. Jesus, reader of souls knew what we were thinking and smiled!

"Teach us how to pray."

Spiritual masters often taught their disciples formulas of praying. The rabbi would give a sample to serve as a model. John the Baptist had done so. Would Jesus?

Jesus had taught His disciples how not to pray by telling the little parable of the Pharisee and the publican. Two men went to the Temple to pray. One, a Pharisee, stood apart by himself and thanked the Lord for not making him like other people, dishonest, adulterers, or like the publican he saw in the corner. He reminded the Lord that he fasted and gave tithes of all he earned. You know that the Pharisees were a devout group who were careful to be observant of the Law, and Jesus recognized the fact that they kept themselves aloof from less observant persons in describing this Pharisee as standing apart, off by himself as he prayed.

The publican was a tax collector and not esteemed by most people. This man, however, was humble and prayed in the shadow, asking God to have mercy on him. Jesus noted that the man who went home justified, that is, at peace with his God, was not the Pharisee but the publican.

Granting His disciples their request, Jesus told them:

"When you pray, use this prayer,

Our Father, who art in heaven, hallowed be Thy name.

Thy Kingdom come.

Thy will be done, on earth as it is in heaven.

Give us this day our daily bread.

Forgive us our trespasses, as we forgive those who trespass against us.

Lead us not into temptation but deliver us from evil."

When we use this prayer, we place ourselves in relation to a Father who loves us, Who is ready to hear us before we even think of praying! He has placed in our hearts the desire to pray!

We ask Him to be with us, to protect and preserve us.

We ask to experience the peace of His Kingdom, the reign of happy harmony.

We ask that His will be done, knowing His will is to share His life with us!

We ask for bread; all we have is His, given us in love.

We ask to be forgiven, to be renewed. When we do the same for others, He is pleased. It is a sure way to obtain forgiveness for ourselves. When we ask forgiveness we are reminded that we too are imperfect and can more easily be compassionate towards others who are also human!

We ask His help when Satan strikes. The devil is stronger than we are and eager to see our pain and our fall. He tempts and tries our faith. A prayer to our Father, and we are safe.

The final prayer we make, not to be led into temptation, is the prayer to be saved from the great trial that would tempt us to lose our faith. We all have trials that tempt us to forget God's care for us, but the tradition of a great trial to stand in our way before the final triumph of all who trust in God lies behind this prayer that Jesus taught His followers, a prayer that helps us to grow stronger in our faith when we ask this help from the Father who's always waiting for us to ask Him and always answers us!,

Jesus once summed up His teaching on the importance of asking for what we need, "ask, and you will receive. Seek, and you will find. Knock, and it will be opened to you."

Underlying all that Jesus taught is the revelation in Him of how much God does truly love us and how He longs for our love. He wants us to be His children, whatever our actual age, as little ones needing and desiring the security of knowing their Father is near. All that Jesus taught about prayer is contained in this concept of love, for love invites our prayer, and love makes our prayer. That is why we experience such contentment when we simply speak with Him as with any friend, when we simply desire His company. Jesus himself surely lived this, for He often spent the night in prayer, that is, being with His Father. He would not have been speaking or listening all the time, for He was a man like us, and He and His Father must have enjoyed each other's company!

FORGIVE!

As He was dying, Jesus prayed for those who were putting Him to death:

"Father, forgive them."

Jesus was doing what He taught us to do. In His ministry He followed a pattern. First, a teaching. Then, an act to show what He meant. His prayer to His Father for those who hated Him is the essence of what He taught:

"You've heard it said: an eye for an eye, a tooth for a tooth, but I tell you: forgive."

I heard Him say this, and I was as startled as everyone was! It was a new and wonderful teaching. My sister, to whom I gave much of my property and who remained Jewish, said she considered Jesus' teaching of limitless and unconditional forgiveness to be the distinguishing mark of His followers.

The Torah did direct Israel to punish offenses with penalties to match the crime. This was necessary in a brutal age, when the poor and the powerless had nothing to defend them. God showed His hand when He appeared to Moses on Sinai. He gave him the Ten Commandments, timeless laws that protect the rights of the weak. Moses was to pass these on to Israel.

The Torah has over six hundred other laws, secondary in relation to the Ten Commandments. These laws answer questions of daily life and worship. They make no distinction between the civil and the religious life of Israel. These two aspects of life were closely bound together in Israel and in other nations.

Jesus, however, was concerned with the soul. The spiritual life was the focus of His teaching. To forgive pertains not to the civil life but to the spiritual.

The case for forgiveness was put before us in the book of the wisdom of Sirach. This book is a compendium of insights put together from his own experiences by an elderly sage in the decades preceding Jesus' coming. The wise man argues:

"You ask God to forgive you, but you refuse to forgive another?"

His point is echoed in a little story Jesus told:

"A man had fallen into heavy debt to his employer, the ruler of a petty kingdom. He begged forgiveness of the debt, and the kindly king forgave it. Minutes later, the former debtor met a fellow servant who owed him a mere fraction of what he had owed the king. Deaf to the man's pleas, he had him and his whole family thrown into prison.

The other servants saw and reported to the king. He called the hard hearted man before him and said:

"I forgave your debt. You should have done the same for the man in debt to you."

The unforgiving man was thrown into prison till the debt should be paid."

How Many Times?

The motive in forgiving is to become what we are meant to be, children of His heavenly Father. If we measure too carefully in giving, and forgiving, we may fall short ourselves. Jesus said:

"With the measure you use to measure it will be measured for you."

Our deeply imbedded legalistic background prompted Peter to ask Jesus:

"How many times do I have to forgive someone? Seven times?"

Jesus surprised Peter and the other disciples when He gave this judgment:

"Not seven but seven times seven!" That is, there is no limit to forgiving....

The Prodigal Son

By way of answering the fear of not being forgiven for sinning against God Jesus told this parable that I'm sure you know:

A man had two sons, his helpers and heirs. Loving and generous, he was an ideal father. Nevertheless, the younger son became restless, yearning to experience the world beyond the confines of his father's farm. He asked for the share that would one day be his.

The father knew he had to let his son learn hard facts of life for himself. He divided the shares he had set aside. giving one third to the younger son, as prescribed in the Torah. With this the young man set out and wandered far from home, while the older brother stayed home and worked.

Free from care and constraint, the youth lived it up. The good times rolled along. While his money lasted, so did his new "friends." When the money ran out, so did they.

After a desperate search, the lad found work, tending pigs for a Gentile. You can imagine his state of mind. Son and heir to a prosperous and observant Jew, he was reduced to caring for unclean animals. We Jews were forbidden to raise pigs or to eat their flesh.

He saw that the pigs were eating better than he was! He made up his mind:

"I'll go back to my father and ask him to forgive me. I'll ask him to take me back as one of his hired men."

The dry wind of late summer stirred the dusty road. The father was at his gate, scanning the horizon, as he had done each day, for many days. He shaded his eyes with his hand, straining to see better. Was it just the hope in his heart, or was that his son?

It was his son, his prodigal son! He ran out into the road and towards him as fast as he could. The boy threw himself at his feet, but the father raised him up and embraced him. The young man tried to speak, but his father began to shout:

"Come here, everybody! My son is back! We have to celebrate!"

This was the father's reaction to his son's repentance. Then Jesus showed the mean spirited, all too common, attitude of the older,"faithful", son:

"While the celebration was at its height, the older brother came in from his work on the farm. He heard the music and the sounds of happy voices. He stopped and asked a servant what was going on. Hearing his brother had come back, he refused to go in.

His father waited for him to join them. After a while he went out and pleaded with him to share their joy. The son complained:

"I've stayed with you and worked. When this son of yours comes back from his life of leisure, his money spent on loose women, you throw a party for him."

Ignoring the reference to "your son," as if he were not the lad's brother, the father told him:

"My son, all I have is yours. We have to celebrate the return of your brother. He was dead. Now he's alive! He was lost. Now he's been found!"

71

Healed, Body and Soul

Peter told us of the first occasion Jesus showed His power to forgive, at Capharnaum:

"On a warm late summer day, Jesus was teaching at home, in the house given Him for His center by a devoted follower. He could rest there only at night. All the day long, men and women came to hear and to be healed. This morning He was teaching the basics concerning repentance and forgiveness.

Four men had come, carrying a paralyzed friend. They hoped Jesus would heal him. It was impossible to get inside, so they climbed up and cut a hole in the roof! They lowered their friend to a spot right in front of Jesus.

Remember: it was Jesus' own roof! How would most men react?

In the settling dust, Jesus' face was wonderful to watch. It showed, in rapid succession, puzzlement, shock, and then delight. He was delighted with the faith of the man's friends. Perceiving the sufferer's heaviness of heart, Jesus freed his spirit:

"Your sins are forgiven."

Some teachers of Torah were standing next to Peter and his brother, Andrew. Peter could sense the shock surging through them. He could almost hear them say to themselves:

"How dare He? Only God can forgive sins."

Jesus also sensed their shock and read their thoughts. Confident of His mission, He spoke to everyone as He addressed the paralytic:

"To show you that the Son of Man has power to forgive sins, I tell you to rise. Take up your bed and walk."

The man rose, healed in body and soul. Remember that healing is a sign of the divine presence.

Unwilling to Repent

Capharnaum saw this sign, and many other signs, that God was present in Jesus, that is, that the Kingdom of God was at hand. Yet, it remained unrepentant. Its strength was also its weakness. Beauty of place. Warmth of weather. It was easygoing but spiritless. It thought: why change? We have paradise here and now.

Long before this, the prophet Jeremiah had remarked: cursed is the one who trusts in human beings, who turns away from the Lord. Jeremiah is much loved now by people but was not in his own time! He complained about this to God himself, for God had dragged him out of his quiet country life to speak on His behalf, to turn the hearts of God's own people back to Him. For all his trouble Jeremiah was denounced and abused and rejected. He was so human, often depressed and unhappy (!), as a man closer to us than many other prophets, sublime as are their thoughts.

When Jeremiah said "cursed be" those who rely on other human beings he was simply speaking from his own experience that instead of being blessed, that is, happy, these seekers are "cursed" that is, unhappy. It was not a wicked wish but rather an observation.

Jesus saw doom ahead for the lovely little town and for its neighbors. They had heard Him teach and seen signs of His healing power, but to no effect. For them the world that lasts was far away. The world that passes was close and tangible.

At the end of His ministry in Galilee Jesus foresaw what would happen to these towns He loved. His voice broke as He said:

"Woe to you, Chorazin. Woe to you, Bethsaida. Woe to you, Capharnaum. If the miracles worked in you had been wrought in Sodom, they would have repented. You are headed for ruin."

Words of vengeance? No. As prophet, Jesus used the words and images traditional in pronouncements of the prophets. The prophets of old, Amos and Jeremiah and others, had called upon Israel to change her ways or suffer woes. They were far from wishing ill for their people but warned them in the strongest language that their choice of living as if this life is everything, all there will be, would lead them to what they least desired, an unhappy existence without God who alone can make us truly and lastingly happy. Jesus did the same.

Jesus' Kindness

I'll share two incidents that I witnessed myself. Both contrast the divine and the merely human reaction to sin. The first took place in Galilee:

"If this Man were really a prophet, He'd know what kind of woman is touching Him."

Simon was thinking this as he watched them, Jesus and the woman at His feet. The wealthy Pharisee had invited the current popular figure to his home. For a sophisticate like himself, it was the thing to do. He was not a good host, however.

Our custom in receiving guests was to pour a bit of fragrant oil on the head and water on the feet of the guest coming in from the dusty street.

73

As a sign of his scant respect for a Man below his own social state, Simon omitted these courtesies for Jesus.

Seeing the slight, I was embarrassed and indignant. I would have left, but for Jesus. He himself took a seat as if He had not noticed His host's bad manners. As He did so, a light wind was felt. A woman, her robes flowing as she moved, had entered.

I see you're surprised. In those times, our social habits allowed uninvited persons to attend a dinner, without eating, when an illustrious person, especially a rabbi, was the guest and expected to speak.

It was not the woman herself that upset Simon. It was that Jesus accepted her touch, since He was of rabbi status. He would render Himself unclean by touching an unclean person. She had thrown herself at His feet and poured precious ointment over them, drying them with her hair.

Jesus saw her humble heart, and He saw the haughty heart of His host. Expected to give a teaching, Jesus spoke to Simon:

"Simon, I have something to say to you."

Simon encouraged Him to speak.

Jesus said:

"She's showing her love. She trusted I would forgive her. Her tears show her repentance. The ointment is a sign of her gratitude to God's forgiving love. I came as your guest, but you gave Me no oil to perfume My head, no water to wash My feet. Since she arrived she's not stopped washing My feet with oil and tears of repentance."

The sinner had shown her love. The "sinless" man had not. He was unkind to his Guest in thought and deed. Love covers over a multitude of sins. It goes hand in hand with faith. Jesus blessed the woman:

"Go in peace, dear. Your faith has covered over your sins."

The second incident took place in Jerusalem, outside the Temple:

Jesus had spent the night on the Mount of Olives. At sunrise He walked down the hill and crossed the Kidron valley to go up to the City. After prayer in the Temple He taught in its courts. A group gathered to hear the Teacher.

While He was teaching, another group arrived to spoil the fresh morning air. At least, that was my thought at the time! The group were Pharisees and some teachers of Torah, as I like to call the scribes. They had brought a woman caught in the act of adultery.

Rigid and relentless, these men of religion had come to trap the Teacher. They knew His teaching on forgiveness. If, as they expected, He should render a rabbinic decision on the side of mercy they could accuse Him. He would be guilty of breaking the Law.

"Rabbi, this woman was caught committing adultery. In the Torah, Moses commands us to stone such a person to death. What is Your judgment?"

It was wearying and disheartening for Jesus. Time and again He was confronted by self righteous and harsh interpreters of Torah. They never tired of trying to snare this gentle Man from Galilee. To indicate His disdain of their pettiness, Jesus bent down and wrote in the sand, that is, He looked at the ground as if writing His thoughts there instead of paying attention to an unwelcome speech. Then, as they stood there waiting, He raised His head and gave His decision:

"Let the one without sin be the first to throw a stone."

They began to move away, one by one. Jesus turned to the woman and asked:

"Where are your accusers? Nobody left to condemn you?"

"Nobody, Sir."

"Nor will I condemn you. Go in peace, but sin no more."

Here, let me say something about excommunication, a dreadful punishment that excludes one from community. Jesus thought in terms of a severing of spiritual ties. He allowed this, but He considered it the choice of the one excluded. When asked by His disciples how they should act if one of their community harmed the group by his or her actions, Jesus advised three steps:

First. Try to persuade the wrongdoer privately. If this does not succeed, try a little group of two or three. If this has no effect, put the matter before the whole community. If the one at fault still refuses to repent:

"Treat them as publicans or heathens."

Jesus permitted His community to excommunicate someone as a last resort, and as in fact reflecting the decision of the one at fault. As I search my memory, from what I myself heard and from what Mary and the chief disciples told me, I am quite certain that Jesus Himself never excommunicated anyone.... Nor did Jesus ever refuse to forgive anyone.

ON THE SABBATH

Jesus and His disciples were walking along a path in the middle of a wheatfield. The grain was ripe and ready to harvest, but that would have to wait one more day. This day was a Sabbath.

The disciples were hungry, so they plucked ears of wheat, rubbed them in their hands and ate them. It was allowed by the Torah. A person could pluck ears of grain in another's field and eat them on the spot. It was forbidden to mow the field, however, on the Sabbath.

Some Pharisees followed Jesus and saw what the disciples were doing. They called to Jesus and complained:

"It's the Sabbath. Your disciples are doing what's forbidden."

For them, to pluck the grain and rub it in one's hands was a form of work. Work was strictly forbidden on the Sabbath. Following a rabbinic method Jesus answered by citing a biblical text that related an event in the life of David, the great hero and model king of Israel. In need of food for his men, David took the bread from the sanctuary that only priests were allowed to eat.

Jesus concluded by leaving a thought for these pious men to ponder:

"The Sabbath was made for man, not man for the Sabbath."

The Sabbath! Essential to Jewish life. An outward sign of inner faith. Gift of God to His people. Recall its origin, according to one of our ancient traditions:

The charming scene in the Torah shows us God working six days to fashion the world. Pleased and satisfied, He rested on the seventh day, the Sabbath. He commanded His people to do the same. For them, the Sabbath would be a day of rest and remembrance.

Jews could conform to many customs of other lands. They could never give up the Sabbath. To question a Sabbath tradition was to question the Sabbath itself, or so it seemed to some people.

The concept of work was the theme. In this regard, Jesus was astounded by an all too general lack of common sense. To give you an example:

The Stooped Woman

One sabbath day Jesus was teaching in the synagogue. A practical means of presenting His message concerning God's hesed, His kindness, presented itself. Looking up from the text Jesus saw a woman so stooped she was unable to stand erect. As best she could, she was looking in His direction. He called to her:

"You are freed from your affliction."

She lifted her head and praised the Lord. She had been bound by Satan, as was commonly believed, for eighteen years. Remember that we all ascribed illnesses to Satan. Since he does hate our human happiness and tries to make us sad at every opportunity, our idea had some basis! In this incident, he was put to flight by Jesus' kindness.

The official of the synagogue, responsible then as now for the proper and decorous flow of the service, scolded Jesus and at the same time reminded the congregation:

"We work six days a week. Come for healing on these six days, not on the Sabbath!"

Answering him and his cohorts, Jesus minced no words:

"How hypocritical. What one of you would not work on the Sabbath to pull your donkey or ox out of a pit? This daughter of Abraham was afflicted for eighteen years. Should we not heal her on the Sabbath?"

They were ashamed. The rest of the congregation was pleased with His words and His works.

Jesus was Angry

Jesus met hardened and unyielding opposition on another Sabbath, also in a synagogue. Some Scribes and Pharisees set a trap for Him. They brought a man into the synagogue who had a withered arm. Would Jesus take the bait they held out? Would He convict Himself of desecrating the Sabbath by an act of healing?

Aware of their scheming, Jesus posed the question:

"Is it a good thing to heal on the Sabbath?"

They made no reply. Stunned at their hardness of heart, Jesus became angry. He asked the man to stretch out his arm, and He healed him. Instead of rejoicing at the good work, the Scribes and Pharisees were more than ever determined to have His life. It was clear to us that they simply hated Him and used the Sabbath as an excuse to plan His downfall.

Who Sinned?

On another Sabbath Jesus and His disciples were strolling in the vicinity of the Temple. They came upon a beggar. The man had been blind from birth. As they halted, Jesus was asked:

"Who sinned, to make him blind? Was it his parents?"

"No one sinned. It's an occasion for Me to show God's glory."

Remember, to show God's glory is to show He's present, among us. Jesus was correcting a tradition that links material misfortune or illness of body to sin. He taught that sin affects the sinner's spirit. It dims the soul's awareness of God's joyful presence.

Jesus then healed the man, using symbolic actions which recalled a primitive tradition that explained in simple, human terms, God's creative work. Imitating the divine work of creating man and woman Jesus moistened dry earth with saliva from His own living body. The clay was now ready for the potter, as on the day God fashioned Adam and Eve and breathed life into them. He touched the sightless eyes with clay and told the man to go and wash his face in the pool of Siloam.

Siloam's waters flow silent but sure from under God's Holy City. To wash there and be healed was to touch the hidden hand of the Giver of life. This ever flowing spring is still there; look to the left of the city, down from the corner of the foundation walls of our ruined Temple.

In the minds of His enemies, Jesus had again desecrated the Sabbath. They vented their rage on the man whose eyes had been opened. They intimated that a sinner had healed another sinner, since any kind of work was forbidden on the Sabbath. The man's simple logic only made it worse:

"I don't know if He's a sinner or not. All I know is: I was blind and now I can see."

Several busybodies among the self righteous took the man to some Pharisees, to receive their judgment on the affair. In the ensuing discussion with the Pharisees , the man became bolder and asked how it was that Jesus could be a sinner and yet able to heal his blindness? Since God does not work through sinners, and the Man did work a miracle of healing, a sign of God's presence, He must have been sent by God.

At that, they threw him out of the synagogue, remarking:

"Born in sin, you presume to teach us?"

Such impertinence from a sinner!

The affair was noised abroad, as everything was in Jerusalem! Jesus heard it and found the man:

"Do you believe in the Son of Man?"

"Who is he, so I can believe in him?"

"He's now speaking with you."

The man's soul was lighted by faith. Seeing with the eyes of the spirit as well as the newly opened eyes of his body, he quickly reacted:

"I believe, Lord."

GOD AND MAN

The final year. It began at Passover in Galilee, and it ended at Passover in Jerusalem. In Galilee, Jesus fed His people with loaves and fishes. In the Holy City, He gave His people His body and blood for food and drink.

In Galilee, Jesus revealed to His friends and disciples that He was the Messiah, the Son of God. In Jerusalem, He revealed this to everyone. In the Holy City He declared:

"The Father and I are One."

The Loaves and the Fishes

It was in Galilee that Jesus gave us a great sign of this union between God the Father and Himself. As God had always fed the sheep of His flock, now Jesus fed us, first, with food for the spirit, food that lasts. Then, He gave us food for the body. Even now, I can relive that day:

Passover was near, but Jesus had not gone up to Jerusalem. He usually did celebrate the great feasts in the Holy City, but this time, He stayed in Galilee. I was there with other disciples.

We were waiting for the return of the missionaries Jesus had sent out to preach and to heal the sick. Now they had come back, tired but happy. To give them a rest, He told us all to get into boats and to row across the lake to the northern shore. I saw wistful looks on the faces of people gathering to hear Him.

The wind from the West slowed our progress. When we arrived at the shore, there they were, waiting! Most other people would have been annoyed, but when Jesus saw them, His heart went out to them. He later told us that they seemed like sheep without a shepherd, so He sat and taught them, feeding them food for the spirit.

He spoke of the kingdom of heaven, where His Father has a place ready for each of us. Hearing His words of hope and promise, we forgot our fatigue. It was late afternoon before anyone thought of eating. By this time, the crowd had grown to nearly five thousand!

Concluding His teaching, Jesus called Philip, the practical one:

"They must be famished. We can't send them away without eating. How will we feed them?"

Philip was embarrassed; He had no idea. Some others broke in and advised Jesus to let the people get their own provisions in the neighboring farms and settlements. After all,the area was not that secluded. Jesus countered:

"Why not feed them yourselves?"

A chorus of voices assured Him there was nowhere enough money in the common purse to feed so many. Jesus had,however, a look on His face that was neither worry nor helplessness. At this point, Andrew came up with a boy and said:

"Here's a lad with the lunch his mother packed for him. He wants You to have it, to help feed the people. Here it is, five loaves and two fishes, not much for so many!"

Jesus thanked the boy for his gift and told us to have the crowd sit in little groups on the thick green grass. Then He took the bread and looked up to heaven and thanked His Father.

He blessed the bread and the fish and broke the food into little pieces. He gave it to us to distribute to the people in their groups. We did. Wonder indeed! I had only a few pieces, and I kept sharing them. They never gave out. We gathered up more than we gave out! We had enough for twelve baskets! This was surely God's way of showing He continued to feed His people (remember the twelve tribes of old Israel fed miraculously in the desert).

Jesus was about to send them home in peace, when someone cried out:

"He's the Messiah! We have our king!"

Others took up the cry, but Jesus shook His head and turned away. Then, the very people who'd just wanted to make Him their king turned against Him, muttering mean words. Even some of His disciples joined the grumblers....

What caused Jesus to refuse recognition that He was the One to come, the Messiah? He had acknowledged the fact, privately, to His disciples. It was not only that He saw the materialistic bent of their acceptance. It was that the public proclamation must be made in Jerusalem.

Walking on the Water

Most of us headed home, but Jesus asked the small inner core of His disciples to wait in a boat offshore. He would go and pray by Himself. He needed His Father's reassurance. Peter told me what happened that night:

Peter and the others were in the boat, keeping close to the shore, to watch for Jesus. Night fell, but He had not come. They began to strain at the oars, for the west wind had swung northwards. It was now quite strong and contrary. In spite of it, they kept their post.

Very early in the morning, before the light, they saw Jesus coming towards them, walking on the water. Was He still alive, or was it a ghost? Had His erstwhile supporters found Him and killed Him? As He came closer, it looked as if He would pass them by. They cried out in fear. He said:

"Don't be afraid. It's I."

Peter called to Him:

"If it really is You, have me come to You on the water."

"Come," Jesus said.

At His voice, Peter stepped into the water, but the power of the wind took away his faith. He began to sink, and he called for help. Jesus took him by the hand. As they got into the boat, the wind died down.

Jesus reproved Peter for his lack of faith. This scolding proved to be an infusion of faith for Peter. Later that same day, he would be there for his Friend when he was most needed. I'll tell you about this moving incident:

Soon after sunrise we walked to Jesus' favored place for teaching. It was for me a vision of what the garden of Eden might have been! This late spring day the grass was still bright green and thick. The nearby lake and the green wooded hills behind it made one think of the One who'd made it all.

The Bread of Life

The morning was fresh from the rain in the night, and it was warm and mild. The atmosphere, however, was chilly, filled with an almost tangible discontent. Many of the rebels of the day before had come. Why? I wondered. Be that as it may, they were there.

We sat to hear His teaching. It centered on the significance of the bread He had multiplied on the day before. Going to the heart of it all,

Jesus urged us to seek the bread that lasts forever, the bread given by God through His Son.

We believed His word, because of the miracle He had worked. He was for us a spiritual bread, nourishing us. More than this was beyond our understanding at the time.

The malcontents were not the least interested in knowing what He meant. They asked Him for a sign to prove His teaching, in spite of the sign He'd already given the day before. They wanted a sign to keep them loyal, as Moses had given our ancestors the bread from heaven, the manna in the wilderness.

Jesus replied:

"It was not Moses who gave them bread from heaven. It was My Father. I Myself am the bread from heaven. If you eat this Bread, you will live forever."

They began to ridicule Him. Patiently, Jesus explained. If we are nourished with bread from heaven, we are prepared for its life, eternal life. When they asked Him to give them this food, He said:

"The bread I will give is My flesh."

They stared at Him in disbelief and horror. He continued:

"If you eat My flesh and drink My blood you will have eternal life, and I will raise you up on the last day.

My flesh is food indeed, and My blood is drink indeed. If you eat My flesh and drink My blood, you live in Me, and I live in you."

Most of the people, many of them disciples, got up and left. They had wanted a liberator messiah. They wanted freedom but not the freedom Jesus offered. Besides this, the Nazarene was saying things too barbarous for the ears of civilized persons.

Jesus watched them walk away. Only a few of us were left. I must confess: what He said was beyond my own reasoning, but Peter answered for me and His friends when Jesus asked him:

"Will you leave Me, too?"

Peter answered:

"Where would we go? You speak to us of eternal life."

We stayed because He addressed our deepest desire and need. We all longed to live forever, and we loved Him. We did not understand the great mystery He revealed, but we believed in Him. He was a Man unlike any man I ever met. We could not leave Him.

At the pool of Bethesda

Seven weeks later, Jesus was in Jerusalem. It was a Sabbath, and it was the feast of Weeks (Pentecost). Passover celebrates the spring harvest of barley, and the gift of freedom from the bondage of Egypt. Counting seven weeks or fifty days later, Pentecost celebrates the summer harvest of wheat, and the gift of God's Torah on Sinai.

Pentecost, Passover, and Sukkoth were the pilgrim feasts. On these three feasts every Jew within walking distance was to go up to Jerusalem as a pilgrim. The ultimate goal was the Temple, on these feasts and on the feast of its dedication, Hanukkah.

In the Temple, on each of these feasts, Jesus openly declared He was the One who was to come. In Galilee, He had shown signs He was the Messiah. In His Father's house, He would proclaim Himself to be His Son.

On Pentecost, when the revelation of God's word on Sinai was celebrated, Jesus first revealed His divine origin in a public way, for all to hear:

The sun was rising behind Him as Jesus walked through the eastern gate to the city. He had come down the Mount of Olives, from Bethany, along the road you just used. He had been staying with His much loved friends, Martha, Mary, and Lazarus. Now He was on His way to the Temple, to pray to His Father.

Instead of going there directly, He turned to the right, towards the twin pools of Bethesda, old reservoirs for the nearby Temple. Before His Sabbath prayer, His Father had a work for Him to do. God wanted to honor a popular local legend:

It was widely held by common folk that from time to time an angel came and stirred the waters of Bethesda. The first one into the pool after the angel's visit was healed. This lovely Sabbath day, God sent His Son to visit the pool.

Gentiles too revered Bethesda as place of healing. On His way, Jesus passed a shrine Roman soldiers had dedicated to Serapis, god of healing. Of course, the more observant Jews, myself included, avoided the place. What I'm about to tell you was told me by a scribe I knew fairly well. His curiosity led him to follow Jesus right up to the pool, while we waited outside.

The edge of the pool was crowded with the crippled and the paralyzed. They all seemed to have someone to help them. Jesus noticed a man of middle age whose thin, patched tunic partially hid his helpless legs. He was all by himself, looking at the water. The Healer of souls saw one bruised by years of suffering.

The hope in his heart showed on his face as Jesus bent down and asked:

"Do you want to be healed?"

"I've nobody to help me. When the angel comes, someone always gets there ahead of me."

"I'll help you. Rise, pick up you mat and walk."

The man got up, strode into the street and hurried to the Temple to give thanks. Jesus blended into the crowd, and we made our way to the Temple. The scribe followed the man and saw him accosted by other scribes on their way to worship:

"It's the Sabbath. You're not allowed to carry that mat."

"But I've been healed. The Man told me to pick up my mat and walk."

"What man?"

"I don't know His name."

Dismissed with disdain, he went on his way. Happy to use once useless legs, he strolled about the courtyards, stopping at the great portico of Solomon. This high, pillared porch once ran along the eastern wall of the Temple area, right there in front of us. See the lower walls that used to support it? As on every Sabbath, priests and scribes expounded the Torah there to groups gathered to hear a favorite or famous teacher.

We arrived about the same time as Jesus, and others joined us to hear Him. He had just begun to teach when He saw the man standing at the edge of the group, a grateful look on his face. He interrupted His teaching and went to him, giving a word of wisdom:

"Take care of yourself. Keep God in your life; otherwise you'll experience suffering far worse than what you had."

Worshipers recognized Jesus and asked the man what He had said. Learning the name of his Healer, the former paralytic ran to tell the scribes, thinking they would be pleased:

"It was Jesus who healed me."

They were not pleased. Hurrying to the portico, they upbraided Him in front of His disciples and students. He had broken the Sabbath and caused someone else to do the same. The nearby priests and scribes stopped their own teaching to listen.

I had heard several Sabbath debates between Jesus and teachers of Torah. He always used rabbinic reasoning, the method they employed. For example, Jesus once pointed out to His critics that any man would labor hard on a Sabbath to pull an ox out of a pit. Rabbinic tradition allowed it.

On another Sabbath He reminded them that circumcision, a work, was permitted on a Sabbath.

On this Sabbath, Jesus spoke on a higher level. What I heard Him say was breathtaking:

"My Father is always working, and I too must work."

Priest and scribe stared in horror. In case of real necessity, a man might work on a particular Sabbath. God alone has the right to work on any Sabbath. He alone is always working. They thought, "what sort of man is this? Who but the devil would dare?"

Reading their thoughts, Jesus assured them:

"The Son can do nothing of Himself. I only do what I see the Father do."

What He claimed was clear: He was no demonic rival to God but His Son! He claimed to see the God no human could see without dying.

Jesus shocked them still more by associating Himself with the divine work of giving and restoring life:

"As the Father gives life, so does the Son give life."

They picked up stones to cast at Him, but He faced them down and asked:

"I've done many good works. For which work do you want to stone Me?"

They answered:

"It's not because of a good work. It's because You're only a man, but You're placing Yourself on God's level, as His equal."

Jesus argued that His works should be enough to prove His provenance. Teachers of God's Torah should come to know God Himself. They should recognize Him whenever and however He appears. They should recognize His works and therefore accept the declarations made by the One who performs the works.

Jesus returned to Galilee after this near fatal encounter with priest and scribe at the Temple. Due to a powerful priestly presence and the starkness of its natural surroundings, Jerusalem was more focused on tradition and less open to Jesus than His native Galilee. He spent the summer months preaching and healing, twice raising the dead to life. I'll shortly share these with you but, first, what happened in Jerusalem at Sukkoth.

You never celebrated Sukkoth? For many of our people, it was *the* feast. It was the fall festival, celebrating the memory of the years our forebears wandered in the wilderness, on their way to the land promised them by the Lord. They lived in temporary shelters, "sukkoth," in our ancient tongue, and the Lord watched over them and guided them. We celebrated for eight days.

We who follow Christ no longer keep the Feast, but its meaning lingers and inspires us. It reminds us that this life is a prelude and pilgrimage, to the land of promise: heaven. There, our Father lives, and there Jesus has gone to prepare a place for us. In the meantime, we wend our pilgrim way.

The feast was getting closer, and Jesus' disciples asked Him if He were going to celebrate the feast in Jerusalem, as He usually did. He said He would not go up to the Holy City, and we were not surprised. Rumors of increased tension there had come to us. He told us to go up by ourselves, and we did.

As expected, Jerusalem was tense, and the question was widely circulating: Is He the Messiah? Leaders of the people, priests and Pharisees, were plotting together. Guards were stationed in force in the public places of the Temple precincts. They were to search for Him and seize Him on sight.

We were feasting on figs and fruit of all kinds when James ran in to tell us the news: Jesus was in the City! The Spirit had advised Him to change His mind and go up to Jerusalem. We hurried to the Temple.

It was the eighth and final day of the feast. The theme of this day's celebration was the gift of water in the wilderness, when God ordered Moses to strike the rock from which water gushed forth to satisfy His people's thirst. It had also been a sign of His power for a people of little faith.

In the midst of the celebration, Jesus exclaimed in a loud voice:

"If you are thirsty, come to Me. Living water will well up in your heart."

It was daring! A clear reference to the source of living water, God Himself. Once again He was answering the question of the day: was He the One who was to come? At the time, we could relate Jesus' words to a tradition that thought of God's prophets as dependable springs of water for thirsty souls. They were the channels of His caring for His flock.

Later, with the gift of the Spirit, we could see that Jesus spoke of the spring of living water which is the Spirit. A spring to keep our souls from drying up.

Jesus noticed the Temple guards sent to seize Him. He saw they were paying attention to what He said, and He addressed them, too. He knew them as men of the people, part of that common folk little esteemed by the elite. In their turn, the Guards saw something of God's aura in Him.

The Guards went back to the Sanhedrin without Him. When the Great Council found fault with this, they answered:

"We never heard anyone speak like that before."

The Good Shepherd

Some weeks later, Jesus was again in the Temple. It was winter, and the feast of Hanukkah brightened the darker days. We used to call it the feast of lights. It celebrated the restoration of light to the Temple three hundred years ago.

Enemies of our people had sought to destroy us as a nation. They profaned God's own dwelling place, putting out the light of its lamps. Heroes of our race, the priestly Maccabees, rose and led the Jews to victory over these fearful foes. The lamps of the Temple were lighted again.

The light was a sign of God's presence among his people. At Hanukkah, the courts of the Temple glowed with light. Great torches and myriads of lamps blazed, looking from afar like a beacon to show the way to God's house. In this setting, Jesus declared:

"I am the light of the world."

He was telling them: I am the beacon that lights the way to the Father. Follow this light, and you will find life. He was God's answer to the prayer so often made in this very Temple, "send forth Your light and Your truth. Let these be my guide. Let them lead me to Your holy mountain."

He was also telling them: I am the Messiah. Those learned in the Law commonly refered to the Messiah as "light."

Now, Jesus led these learned leaders towards the light. He wanted them to see for themselves that He was the Messiah, and the Son of God. Following the current way of teaching, He posed this question:

"Who do you say the Messiah is? Whose son is he?"

They replied, "David's."

The scholars of the Scriptures were in agreement, that the messiah was to be a descendant of David. Some thought of a physical descent, others of a spiritual succession. The messiah would be another David, of the same mold, a shepherd and savior of his people.

Then, Jesus planted this seed of thought: the Messiah must be more than merely a son of David. David composed the psalm that commemorates the anointing of king messiah. Jesus used this psalm in His argument:

"If David says in the psalm: the Lord said to my lord, sit at My right, how can David be the father of the Messiah, whom he calls "Lord?"

Jesus meant to make them think. Instead, they shut out the light He gave them. They repeated their question, not at all interested in whether He was in fact the Messiah but rather in getting Him to say so. Then they could accuse Him of being a pretender and imposter.

"Tell us, plainly, are You the Messiah?"

Jesus saw their plot and reminded them:

"I've told you."

Indeed, He had told them, many times and in many ways. He had healed the sick and raised the dead. He had proclaimed the good news of the Kingdom. He had told them He was the light of the world. They refused to see the glory of God shining in front of their eyes. They did not want to hear Him say:

"I am the Good Shepherd."

This was yet another way of saying, "I am the Messiah, the anointed one."

He also identified Himself as God, for the good, that is, the authentic shepherd of Israel is God Himself. Through the ages, our people have prayed:

"We are Your people, the sheep of Your flock."

Before Israel herself had an anointed one, the kings of the peoples who surrounded her boasted of being first of all shepherds of their people. Once Israel too had an anointed one, David the ideal king, he tended her as a shepherd tends his flock. For centuries following, Israel waited for another messiah to take David's place as a good shepherd.

The good shepherd knows his sheep, and the sheep know the voice of their shepherd. Since the Father and He are One, the voice of Jesus is the voice of God, Israel's shepherd. Moreover, as David once boasted of risking his own life to save his sheep, Jesus announced He was to lay down His own life for His sheep.

This was Jesus' final discourse in the Temple. As His opponents again took up stones to threaten Him, He turned from them and walked out of the Temple.

Remember the prophecy of Ezekiel, as he described the divine presence leaving Israel's temple? This time, the divine presence would leave the temple as a limited dwelling place but only to be with all of us and each of us during our days on earth, drawing us, helping us, to one day dwell with Him forever in His heavenly home....

THE LORD OF LIFE

Just days before He died, Jesus entered Jerusalem as Messiah. He had refused this public demonstration in Galilee, for that was not the designated place. Nor had the time arrived. Now, both place and time were at hand. The hour was near for the depth of divine love to be revealed.

As a sign God's will was to be fulfilled, Jesus made two dramatic gestures in the manner of the prophets of old. He entered David's city as scion of his royal house. Then, He cleansed the Temple, His heavenly Father's holy house.

Triumphal Entry into Jerusalem

The day of His entry into Jerusalem was glorious! The weather was clear and fresh, and the sunshine matched our mood. We were on our way to the Holy City from Bethany. If you go to the top of this hill, you'll see that place so loved by the Lord. I'll tell you more of this later, but now I'll narrate the events of that day:

By the time we reached Bethphage, midway between Bethany and where we are now, a considerable number of people had joined us. Jesus stopped and asked two of His disciples to go and get a donkey in Bethany. If anyone should ask why they were taking the donkey, they were to say its Owner needed it.

It sounded mysterious, but the disciples went on the errand without a question. I happened to know exactly what Jesus meant; the day before, we were dining at Bethany, in the house of His friends. I was chatting with Jesus when another guest, one of their neighbors, came up to Him. He had noticed Jesus had no donkey to ride and offered Him one not yet ridden. He would keep it for Jesus' use, whatever He wished.

The two disciples soon returned with the donkey. Jesus swung Himself up and sat there, looking towards the Holy City. As He did, everyone began to shout, "King Messiah!"

They cut branches from nearby trees. Waving them and singing, we made our way down this Mount and up into the city. Waving the branches reminded me of Sukkoth, when we waved branches to recall God's leading our forebears to this Land. This day, however, we were celebrating the coming of His Son, the long awaited Messiah.

The crowd had swelled to some hundreds by the time we reached the eastern gate to the city. We were singing the song of the Messiah:

"Hosanna, Son of David! Blessed is he who comes in the name of the Lord!"

Do you know the background to what we were doing and the song we sang?

It's from the time of Israel's return from the Babylonian captivity. Our forebears were discouraged by the problems of rebuilding their city and its temple. It seemed too much for them. At this point, the Lord sent word to them through the prophet Zechariah.

The prophet foretold a time of relief and the coming of the Messiah. This is what he promised Israel:

"Shout aloud, daughter of Jerusalem! Look, your king is coming to you...humble, riding a donkey...he shall banish war horses from Jerusalem... his rule shall extend from sea to sea...to the ends of the earth!"

The city was filled with pilgrims. Some had heard of Jesus, some had not. As we entered, people asked what was happening. When we told them it was Jesus of Nazareth, some of them joined us. For some reason, I remember a lull in the singing and shouting. The only sound was the whish of the branches.

Common folk proclaimed Him Messiah. Great ones plotted His death. The chief priests saw in Him a threat to their authority, to their very livelihood. What Jesus now did and said seemed to confirm their fear:

Jesus Cleanses the Temple

We were walking in the court of the Gentiles, the vast open space of the Temple precincts open to non-Jews. Less sacred than the inner courts, it had become a busy place of trade. Only Jewish coins could be used in the Temple, so money changers had tables in the court of the Gentiles. For the convenience of those who wished to offer animal sacrifice, dealers in livestock had set up stalls with sheep and doves.

Traders were calling out their bargains to the men and women on their way to worship. This had always been distracting to me. I reasoned: this court is less sacred than the inner courts, but it's still within the precincts of God's holy house. The trading seemed to me to violate the holiness of God's temple.

Jesus showed I shared His sentiments:

It happened without warning. One of the traders called to Jesus Himself. Jesus whirled around and advanced on the man's table. At any time, Jesus was impressive, strongly built, taller than average, His face striking to behold. Only large groups dared confront Him. The trader fled.

Overturning the table and seizing a rope, Jesus swung it in the air for attention. By this time, the noise of the voices had stopped and trading ceased. All eyes were on Him as His voice rang out:

"Get these things out of here! How dare you turn My Father's house into a place of trade?"

A Semite through and through, Jesus had the intensity so characteristic of our race. Never lukewarm, this day the wrath of God so often on the lips of prophets was on the lips of His Son. In fact, Jesus was fulfilling prophecies uttered by the last of the prophets of old, Zechariah and Malachi.

Pious Jews, including myself, knew these prophecies from long hours of childhood memorizing. The priests, of course, knew them,too. They were filled with fury at Jesus' words:

"What right have You to do these things?"

A prophetic word was His answer:

"Destroy this Temple, and in three days I will raise it up."

By "this Temple," Jesus meant His body, true dwelling of the Lord. After the Resurrection, we understood. At the time, we did not. Neither did the priests. They understood Him to threaten the end of their ministry. This stiffened their resolve to kill Him.

The resurrection of His body would be the sign of His authority. His power over death would prove His authority over everything, including the Temple.

Before His own resurrection, Jesus showed His power over death by raising three persons from the dead.

The third to have life restored was Lazarus, Jesus' friend. Instead of seeing in this miracle a sign of God's glory in His Son, the priests and their allies wanted to kill Lazarus! Before I describe this raising of

Lazarus to life I'll recall for you the other two miracles that both occurred in Galilee:

The Daughter of Jairus

The first took place not far from Capharnaum. An official of the synagogue, Jairus, came and asked Jesus to save his dying daughter. Jesus said He would go home with him. We all went, quite a crowd, in fact.

On the way, a woman in need of healing saw her opportunity. We saw what happened, but the woman later filled in details for us:

For twelve long years she had suffered a hemorrhage. The physicians had done all they could. It would not stop. She had spent all she could and was on the brink of despair. Then, Jesus came into her life. As He walked along, on His way to the dying girl, she thought:

"If I touch His robe, I'll be healed."

She did, and she was healed.

Jesus was not a passive channel of supernatural power. As she touched His robe, He felt power go out to someone. He turned and saw the woman. Noting her fear, He said:

"Don't be afraid. Your faith has healed you. Go in peace."

Just then, someone came to Jairus and told him:

"Your daughter has died. Don't trouble the Master further."

Jesus, however, insisted on going to the house. So Jairus sadly led the way. We could hear the keening of the mourners even before we arrived. As Jesus entered, they stopped and stared at Him. Jesus asked:

"What's all this commotion, this weeping? The girl's not dead. She's only sleeping."

They laughed in His face, because they had no idea of what He meant, nor of His power. He meant, of course, that her death was not final. It was a sleep from which she would awake. He put them all out of the room, allowing only Peter, James, and John to remain.

He touched the lifeless hand and said:

"Little girl, rise."

She sat up!

Jesus called in her family and asked them to give her something to eat. He knew her weakened body needed some nourishment, and He wanted them to know she was not a ghost.

You noticed He took His three closest disciples with Him to see His power over death. Remember, He had taken these three with Him to see His glory on the mountain. These two revelations of His power and glory prepared them for a third, the extent and depth of divine love. This love was seen in His agony in the garden of Gethsemane.

These three disciples, the core of the Twelve, themselves the core of His church, saw and remembered the three pivotal points of His ministry. They saw and remembered His power and His glory and His love.

The Widow of Nain

The second time Jesus raised the dead to life was in many ways the most moving of all the signs of His authority and power. It happened at Nain:

Nain, the pleasant place, typical of the little towns Jesus loved. It nestled, and still does, against the low hills on the border of Samaria. We had crossed the plain of Esdrelon, coming from Capharnaum on the lake. As we neared the village, we knew something was wrong.

It was the silence. Too late for afternoon rest, too early for evening calm. We should have heard the sound of human voices. For many minutes, we heard nothing at all .

Then, a procession appeared, perhaps the entire village? Still no sound. It was uncanny, the only time I heard no keening at a death and burial. Other times, the shrieks and cries of mourners made a din as if to raise the dead. This time, the grief was obviously too deep for vocal expression.

They were carrying the body of a young man, the only son, as we learned, of a poor widow. Joined to her sorrow was the grim prospect of poverty. He had been her only means of support.

Jesus was deeply affected. He went to the mother and said:
"Don't cry."
He spoke to the youth, as if he were not dead but sleeping:
"Young man. Rise."
He did! Joyful shouts shattered the stillness of death.

Jesus' Friends in Bethany

Now, to the raising of Lazarus:

On His visits to Jerusalem Jesus stayed with friends in Bethany. Perhaps it made Him think of His home at Nazareth? They were about the same size, and both lay on hilly ground. In any case, Jesus found a second home in Bethany, in the house of Simon and his children, Martha, Mary, and Lazarus.

At the top of this hill, look east. You'll see the same sight that delighted Jesus. The pale brown beauty of rounded hills, smoothed by the winds of time, sloping down to the lowest spot we know, the Jordan valley. The heights beyond are the hills of Moab. At their feet is a small patch of deep blue, what you can see from here of the sea without life.

Jesus loved beauty, of nature and of soul. He found both in Bethany. Of an evening He would sit and speak of life without end. Martha and her siblings enjoyed His company and His lessons.

I knew the family well, from business dealings with the elderly Simon and his son, Lazarus. The home was most often spoken of as the home of Martha, as she was the eldest and the housekeeper, and of course, the hostess. Well-to-do and most hospitable, the family was rarely without guests.

Bethany was outside the Holy City, and Simon's family was outside certain circles. Simon was rich and had many friends, but few among the priests and Pharisees. Long cured of quite a serious skin disease. he was still commonly called, "Simon, the leper." Worse than this, perhaps, Mary had always been a free spirit, although now reformed and devoted to Jesus.

Mary was the dreamer, Martha the doer, famed for the table she set. Once I witnessed a good example of the sisters' differing personalities. It was at a dinner for Jesus and a few of His disciples, but with many others crowding the upper room. Martha was bustling about, while Mary sat at Jesus' feet, drinking in His words. Clearing her throat each time she passed her sister, Martha finally interrupted Jesus:

"Tell my sister to help me!"

He told her:

"Martha, you worry about so many things. Only one thing is really needed. Mary has chosen this, and it will not be taken from her."

Attuned to His mind, she quickly understood and sat down to listen. I have often pondered this scene. Jesus' words still echo in my mind. They remind me of other words from a psalm first sung, I think, by David:

"One thing I ask of the Lord, to dwell in His house all the days of my life."

David, God's inspired minstrel, was singing to His Lord, the light and salvation in all his troubles. Rising to a mystic height, he asks to be God's guest, for ages to come. This was the one thing he asked, the one thing Jesus asked Martha to keep in mind.

Another thought came to my mind while I pondered the ancient psalm. Like Martha, David had planned and worried about many things. Among them was his perception that God needed a house, a temple. His divine Friend told David not to worry so much. He would build David a house, that is, a dynasty.

As I ponder the scene at Bethany, it seems to me that Jesus was telling Martha, His hostess, that He would be her Host, to care for her spiritual needs. This is why He wanted her to hear what her sister was hearing. He had things to tell her.

Now, the raising of Lazarus to life! I witnessed the miracle, but what preceded this was told me by John. As I recall:

The Raising of Lazarus

Jesus was on the other side of the Jordan when the message arrived, from Martha and Mary:

"The one You love is ill."

A few faithful followers had come with Jesus to this remote place. They thought He had fled here for fear of His enemies. Threats were now openly made on His life. His retreat to this spot was more in view of preparing Himself for the final test. He knew it was close at hand.

Jesus also knew His friend had already died, but He was speaking of eternal life when He remarked to the disciples:

"This sickness will not lead to death but to the manifestation of God's glory and the glory of His Son."

Listening to his Father's voice, Jesus stayed where He was for two more days. Then He told His disciples:

"Now, let's go to Judea."

They were surprised. It would be walking into a lion's den, for Judea was the center of opposition to Him. His life itself would surely be in danger. Jesus assured them He was walking in the light, that is, His path was clear and guarded by His Father.

Then, He told them:

"Lazarus is asleep. I will go and wake him."

Jesus often spoke of death as sleep, from which the faithful rise again. Without thinking, someone remarked that if he were asleep, Lazarus was on the way to recovery. Jesus said:

"Lazarus has died. For your sakes, I'm glad I was not there, for now your faith will be strengthened."

Twice before, Jesus had raised the dead to life, soon after their death. This time, there was no question. Lazarus was certainly dead. By now, he had been placed in the tomb.

Still thinking of the danger He faced in going to Bethany in Judea, Thomas said:

"Let's go to die with Him!"

I was with Martha and Mary when Jesus arrived. Their brother had died four days before. Mary stayed with the many friends who'd come to console the two spinster sisters whose lives had revolved around the brother everyone loved. Martha hurried to meet Jesus, and some of us followed.

Practical as ever, Martha told Jesus her brother would not have died had He been there. She added, always practical, that she was sure God would honor whatever Jesus wanted to do! It was a strong suggestion. She knew He had restored two others to life. Surely, His friend?

Jesus intended this, but He used the occasion to instruct the growing group:

"Your brother will rise again."

Martha affirmed her belief in the resurrection of the just. Jesus told her He Himself was the resurrection and life, that is, through Him the just will rise to life without end.

"All who believe in Me will live forever, even though they have died. Do you believe this?"

Martha spoke clearly:

"I do. I believe that You are the Messiah, the Son of God, the One who was to come."

Jesus intended to confirm her faith. He would show He was indeed Messiah and Son of God. He would show His power over death. He asked Martha to get Mary, so they could all go together to the tomb.

Mary came. At the sight of her tears, Jesus too began to weep. They walked the short distance up the hill from the town to the tomb. At the tomb, Jesus asked them to roll away the stone. Martha objected; by now there was surely a stench. Jesus insisted.

When the stone was rolled away, Jesus raised His eyes and thanked His Father for always hearing His prayer. Then, He called to His friend:

"Lazarus, come out!"

Responding to the voice of his Friend, Lazarus appeared at the entrance of the tomb, struggling with the burial linens.

The Symbolic Anointing

The sisters gave a supper to celebrate and to thank their Friend. I was among the guests. The ritual for receiving an honored guest, the kiss of peace, the washing of feet, and the anointing of the head with oil, all so symbolic that day. It was His final feast as honored guest, before He died for those He loved.

Martha served His food and drink. Mary washed His feet. She anointed His head with drops of precious oil of nard. The rest, at least two cups' full, she poured on His feet, wiping them dry with her hair. The large room was filled with the fragrance.

Judas commented:

"Such a waste. This expensive ointment could have been sold and the money given to the poor."

Later, John remarked that love of the poor was hardly Judas' motive in criticizing Mary's generosity. He labeled Judas a thief. As money manager for the little community of disciples he used to help himself to the common purse from time to time.

Jesus rebuked Judas on the spot:

"Let her be. She's done this for My burial. You always have the poor with you, but you'll not always have Me."

He was telling Judas He was aware of his plotting. It had no effect. Judas hardened his heart and went to the chief priests with an offer to betray his Friend to them. How much would they give him? Thirty pieces of silver, the price of a slave.

THE NIGHT BEFORE HE DIED

The hot sand-filled wind from the desert had been blowing since shortly after daybreak. As the number of pilgrims who crowded its streets and alleyways rose, the mood of the Holy City fell. Usually, an air of happy excitement filled Jerusalem as the Passover drew near. This day, the warm wind brought fatigue and bad temper. The wind shaded the sun; an early darkness could be expected.

It was two days before the Passover of that year, which fell on a Sabbath. Jesus knew the time had come. He could not wait. He and His friends must eat their Passover meal this very evening.

Word came to Jesus that the Sanhedrin had decided to seize Him this evening, before the feast. The next day, lambs would be slain and the Passover meal would be eaten in the evening. Israel would celebrate the memory of the night the Lord freed her from bondage to Egypt. This year, the Lamb of God would be slain to free the world from bondage to sin.

He told the Twelve they would have their Passover meal this night, the day before the common Passover. When they asked where, He sent Peter and John into the city. He had arranged everything:

"You'll see a man carrying a water jug. Follow him. Where he stops, ask the owner of the house to show you a room you can prepare for us. Tell him the Master must eat His Passover this night. Prepare the room for us."

In the early evening, Jesus and the Twelve went to the upper room, readied for their feast of friendship. Jesus' heart was heavy with dread, but He wanted to give His life for His friends. Before I continue, remember that the Twelve disciples were not only the core of Jesus' community. They represent all of us who are His followers and His friends, His spiritual family. We show this when we hear and heed His words.

I was not there, but it almost seems as if I were! Many times Peter, and James, and John told me what He said and did. I can hear the familiar voices. I can feel the fear and foreboding that filled the room.

Jesus had been looking forward to this supper, the climax of the many meals they'd had together. Yet, as soon as they entered the upper room His disciples disappointed Him. His teaching onhumility had not taken root; they began to dispute the best places!

When they were all seated, Jesus began to teach them. His theme was love. The starting point was the lack of humility they had just shown! He reminded them that love is humble, thinking of the other more than of self.

As usual, Jesus combined word and deed. To their great consternation, He put on an apron, as would a slave. Then, He knelt by each one and washed their feet. When his turn came, Peter said:

"You'll never wash my feet!"

Jesus looked up into his face and told him:

"If I do not wash your feet, you cannot share My life."

Peter exclaimed:

"Then, not only my feet but my hands and head as well!"

Jesus made him to understand that what He was doing was a symbolic gesture. It was meant to signify a purifying of the heart, to enable the disciples to share Jesus' life, both human and divine. It was also meant to signify the self humbling of God in His Son, stooping down to help His helpless children. Jesus asked His disciples to show such humble service to one another.

Looking back, the Twelve could see this foot washing as the first part of His setting them apart to carry on His mission. His mission had begun with His baptism in the Jordan and the descent of the Spirit upon Him. Now, they were washed clean and now they could receive His Spirit after His rising from the dead.

First, they shared His body and blood.

At a previous Passover in Galilee, Jesus showed His power by feeding five thousand people with a few loaves and fish. After this He promised to feed us more wondrously, with His own body and blood. Fulfilling this promise, He took bread and declared:

"This is My body."

At the end of the meal, He took a cup of wine and said:

"This is My blood."

He directed them to:

"Do this in memory of Me."

They shared the Bread and the Cup. Jesus explained that the Cup was His blood to seal the Covenant. This was new.

The commitment to a covenant is sealed by blood, the sign of life. At Sinai, God accepted the offering of animal blood to seal Israel's commitment to the covenant. Now, Jesus offered His own blood to seal the covenant. The blood was physical, but the sharing is mystical, transcending time and space.

With the new covenant a new command is given. It is the old command of love but in a new setting, one without limits, the model given by Jesus' offering of Himself.

"A new command I give you: love one another, as I have loved you."

This love can be commanded. It is not the natural love we have for certain persons. It is really supernatural, sometimes very difficult, as we try to see others as God does ! We may not like certain people, let alone their words and deeds, but Jesus commanded us to love them, as He does. He certainly does not like everything we say and do, but He loves us. We need His help!

"Do this in memory of Me," repeats His words and His love. When His words, "this is My body; this is My blood," are pronounced with faith, He is present with His saving act of love. When we love one another He is present.

This new command is the only command Jesus gave. It sums up all the commands given or sanctioned by God. Some accused Jesus of trying to alter the Torah. On the contrary, He fulfilled it by word and deed.

Judas

I'm not sure of the sequence here. Peter insisted that Judas had left before the first Eucharist, but others were equally certain he left only after eating and drinking the heavenly food. In any case,

Jesus interrupted His teaching to say:

"One of you will betray Me."

Eleven of the Apostles were shocked. They began to ask each other whom Jesus could mean.

Someone asked Jesus Himself. He answered:

"I'll dip a piece of bread and give it to him."

He dipped the bread and gave it to Judas. This was a mark of special favor, as you know. What did Jesus have in mind? Was He showing Judas He loved him, in spite of what He knew?

The betrayer asked:

"Am I the one?"

In a voice faint from fatigue, and sorrow, Jesus said:

"You can answer your own question."

Then, He raised His voice:

"What you are going to do, do it now."

Judas got up and went out into the darkness of night.

You might ask: how could he do such a thing? How could he live with such a beautiful person and not return His love? How could Jesus continue to love Him, as He obviously did?

I don't know the answers, nor did the other Eleven.

To conclude the sad story of Judas:

At the sight of Jesus suffering, He did repent his betrayal. He tried to return the thirty pieces of silver to the Sanhedrin. They refused to take it, so he threw the money on the ground and went off to hang himself.

In that moment between life and death did he also accept the forgiving love of his Lord? I like to think so.

After Judas had left, Jesus spoke of His own departure. He wanted to prepare them for His absence, saying they could not come with Him at this time. Peter spoke for everyone when He asked:

"Where are You going?"

Jesus repeated:

"Where I am going you cannot come now, but you will follow Me later."

Peter's Denial Foretold

"Why can't I follow You now? I'm ready to die for You."

"Are you ready to die for Me?"

Jesus knew Peter loved Him, but He saw the events that lay ahead that very night. He saw that fear would overcome Peter's courage. It was to be, for He was to die alone. Peter had to stay behind, to lead His flock and to remember....

Jesus prepared Peter for the traumatic experience he was to have that night. He told him bluntly:

"Before the cock crows to announce the day you will insist you don't even know Me."

Peter was confused. So were the others. What Jesus now said was even more confusing for them.

"Whoever sees Me sees the Father"

He told them not to be afraid. He was going to leave them but only to prepare rooms for them in His Father's house. Later, He would come back for them, and they would be with Him. He assured them they knew the way.

Thomas asked:

"We don't know where You are going. How can we know the way?"

Jesus answered:

"I am the way. Nobody comes to the Father except through Me."

He added that He is truth, the Father's mind and heart revealed. All that we search for and need in life has been revealed in Him. He is life itself, that is, everything we need for true and unending life is found in Him. He shows us by word and by deed how deeply and faithfully God loves us.

Philip asked:

"Show us the Father, and that will be enough."

Jesus answered:

"Philip, by now you should know; whoever sees Me sees the Father."

All we need to know, and can know, about God is revealed in His Son. Jesus is the Father's perfect image. Until Jesus came, God's heart was shrouded in sacred mystery. In His Son, in His ministry and on the cross of Calvary, God bared His heart before His own creation.

Another Helper

The disciples were becoming more apprehensive. Jesus encouraged them. He was to leave them physically, but He promised to send another Helper and Guide. This Guide would be with them spiritually, in their hearts:

"Don't be afraid. I'll not leave you orphans. I'll send you another helper, to be with you, the Spirit. He'll stay with you forever. He'll remind you of all I've told you."

The Spirit. Jesus had revealed that God is Father and Son. Now He revealed that God is Father and Son and Spirit. I say Jesus revealed the Spirit's place, but we did not understand it at the time; this came on the occasion when the gift of Jesus and His divine Father came to us, as Jesus promised. Then we could see.

With the Spirit's help Jesus' disciples reflected through the years on what He said that night. This the fruit of their reflection:

The Spirit is the Spirit of the Son and of the Father. Unlike your spirit and my spirit, the Spirit of the Father and of the Son is a distinct Person. Distinct Persons, they are united in a bond of love so perfect they are never separated.

"Remain in My love."

To remain in His love is to share His life. If we do, He is with us now in uncertainties and in our pain, and we will be with Him one day in the unending happiness of His divine life! If we abide in His love, we gradually come to know Him so intimately that we sense His thoughts. He is planning our happiness.

Jesus summed this up:

"If you remain in My love, ask what you want, and it will be yours."

The love that unites the Father and the Son and the Holy Spirit will be ours! If Jesus had not revealed this, we would never be able to imagine such a gift! To ponder this is to have the peace Jesus promised His disciples as His parting gift:

"Peace is what I leave you. My own peace is what I give you. I do not give it as the world gives."

Then, He rose from table and invited them to go with Him to Gethsemane. They often went there in the evenings, when the grotto and the olive garden were empty. They would go there and pray.

THE PASSION

That night was very warm, and the air was filled with the fragrance of orange blossoms. I could smell them even inside my house, as I lay on my bed. The valley here below us was then a little Eden of orange trees. I have forgotten many details, even the actual sequence of what happened that night, but the strong sweet scent of those flowers is with me still.

My house was not far from this orange garden. It was to the left of those huge stone slabs. These immense stones were part of the vast outer wall of the Temple Jesus knew. As you see, this area is now only ruins. For the few years Mary lived in Jerusalem with me we used this house.

Soon after she died and was taken into heaven, the great revolt of our people began. Most of the community of His followers fled the city, which was besieged and destroyed.

The ruins hide the site of my house and the stepped street that led past it down to this fruitful Kidron valley. The ruins also hide the great gate that led into the Temple precincts. I presume that gateway is still there under the tumble of debris. Many times all of us, Jesus too, passed under its arches and into the courtyards of the Temple.

Gethsemane

I tried to sleep, but the heaviness in the air kept me awake. I was at last about to drop off to sleep when I heard voices, loud, actually shouting. I sat up and listened. As they came closer, moving down the street in the direction of Gethsemane, I heard what they were shouting: for Jesus' death!

Given its use by devoted friends, I think His friends in Bethany but no longer remember, Jesus often used the garden and its grotto to meet with His inner core of disciples. It is at the foot of this hill where we're now standing.

107

I grabbed a sheet and wrapped it around me as I dashed into the street, down the steps and across the bridge to the garden. There I saw a group of armed men, a mixture of riffraff, Roman soldiers, and Temple guards. They were pressing together at the entrance to the olive garden.

What I saw I can never forget. Jesus was standing just inside the entrance to the garden, facing the crowd. At the head of the crowd was Judas. This false friend walked up to Jesus and kissed Him. Jesus asked him:

"Judas, you betray the Son of Man with a kiss?"

What happened in the garden before this tragic scene I heard from Peter. The trauma of that night misted his memory, and the memory of the other disciples, so that they forgot the exact sequence of what transpired. They never forgot the experience itself. This is what happened before I arrived:

When they reached the place, Jesus asked His eleven friends to stay with Him while He prayed. He took Peter, and James, and John with Him further into the garden. He wanted them nearby, to receive the help He was asking of His Father for endurance in what lay ahead.

Hearts heavy from strain, the three disciples fell asleep. They had tried to keep awake, but even Peter drifted off. He could hear Jesus weeping and praying:

"Abba, You can do anything. Take this cup away from Me."

After a pause, Jesus said firmly:

"I will do what You want Me to do."

Suddenly, Peter felt Jesus' hand on his shoulder. Looking up into His face, Peter saw with horror that He had sweated blood. Jesus said to them:

"Sleeping? Can't you stay awake and watch with Me? Stay awake and pray for endurance."

He went back and knelt a short distance from them. Peter again tried to stay awake. Eyes drooping from exhaustion, he saw a ghostly figure appear at the side of Jesus, comforting Him. The next thing he knew, Peter felt the touch of Jesus' hand on his shoulder. He had slept again. This time Jesus said:

"Get up, now. It's time. My hour has come."

They could hear the rumble of voices and see the glow from the approaching torches. Jesus calmly waited for the mob to arrive. Peter and James both had swords, but Jesus ordered them sheathed. He said:

"Whoever lives by the sword dies by the sword."

Nevertheless, when they arrived, Peter unsheathed his sword. Malchus, one of the High Priest's slaves, was well known to us, a swaggering bully. As he moved to seize Jesus, Peter struck with his sword. Malchus swerved to avoid the blow, but his ear was almost severed.

Jesus healed it. He meant to show us that violence cannot be met by violence. That was His firm teaching. He also wanted to show that He intended to drink the cup He had freely accepted.

He confronted His foes, demanding they name the One they were seeking. They replied:

"Jesus of Nazareth."

Jesus told them:

"I am He. Why did you not arrest Me during the day, when I was openly teaching in the Temple? Why come in the dark of night? Am I then a criminal?"

The unruly mob fell back, awed by the miracle of Malchus' ear and by Jesus Himself. They had no answer. Then the power of the night reasserted itself, and they seized the Lord of light. His disciples all fled.

I stood and stared. My brain refused to accept what my senses saw and heard. I saw Peter and the others flee, but still I stood there. I came out of my shock when I felt a tug at the sheet wrapped around me. Two of the guards had grabbed me by this sheet.

My only thought was to get away. With my free arm I gave one of the guards a blow that sent him reeling. As the other guard loosened his grip to use his sword, I easily slipped out of the sheet. I left it in his hand and fled into the dark.

I ran across the Kidron and up the steps of the darkened street. Fear and physical condition got me to my door without stopping. I found the door as I had left it, closed but not bolted. I had escaped.

I washed and dressed myself. The air had quickly cleared, and the night had turned cold. This helped to calm my mind and form a resolve to see what was happening.

I heard the sound of the crowd coming back up the street. I waited till they'd passed my house. When I opened the door, Peter and John were walking by. They were dazed and did not even see me. I followed them.

Most of Jerusalem was still asleep, safe and secure behind the doors it had closed. The door to the great house of Annas the priest was open, to those the gatekeeper knew. It meant nothing to her if a person was a disciple or not. She knew James and John but not Peter.

John persuaded the gatekeeper to let Peter in. James came along just afterwards and went right in. Most of what I'm now narrating I heard from him.

Jesus Before The Priests and the Sanhedrin

In the large courtyard members of the Sanhedrin were seated around Annas. Let me explain:

The Sanhedrin was a group of seventy elders who constituted a sort of supreme council and court for the Jewish people of our homeland under the leadership of the high priest. Annas was not the official high priest that year. He had been high priest, appointed, according to our tradition, for life. To show their power, the Romans had deposed him and appointed a succession of others to the office. Five of these were Annas' own sons. The present chief priest was his son-in-law, Caiphas.

Annas and his sons were still considered "chief priests" by the other priests and the Sanhedrin. These chief priests and the official chief priest, Caiphas, regarded Annas as the ultimate religious authority. Jesus was first brought before him.

The trial was a travesty, for it was at night. There was no authority for either priest or Sanhedrin to conduct a nocturnal enquiry. It was done in haste, to get rid of Jesus before the feast. They would do their work in the dark.

Jesus stood before Annas and the rulers of the people. They and their witnesses sat in the shadows. They had placed Him in the light of the flickering fire. James told me he never forgot the stillness.

There was not a sound. Were they waiting for Annas to speak? Did a sense of shame prevail for a fleeting moment? Perhaps it was nature itself, shocked into silence?

Peter moved closer to the fire to warm himself. The very girl who had let him in now stared at him and said:

"You're one of His, aren't you?"

He denied any association with Jesus, edging away from the fire and its light. Even then, other servants turned to look at him. At least twice again, someone insisted Peter must be a follower of Jesus. One was sure he'd seen him with Jesus earlier, in the garden. Another asserted:

"You must be one of His. You're a Galilean."

Again Peter lost his nerve. He swore he did not even know Jesus! After the third denial, Jesus turned and looked at him.

I was standing by the gate and heard the cock crow, announcing day was near. A moment later, Peter came out. He was a man of strong emotions, but I had never seen him weep. Now I saw him weeping bitterly.

Inside the courtyard, it was still night. The High Priest and Sanhedrin were anxious to finish before daybreak. When it was light they would send Jesus to Caiphas, for his approval. He in turn would send Jesus to the Roman procurator, Pontius Pilate, for they wanted Jesus' death but did not have the authority to carry out capital punishment. The Romans had reserved this to themselves..

Pilate was privy to the dark deed. Well informed, he knew that the priests and their allies were jealous of Jesus. Yet he allowed Roman soldiers to take part in Jesus' arrest.

If Jesus' enemies could prove Him a threat to the public order, the Romans would rid them of this Galilean. For their witnesses, the chief priests and the majority of the Sanhedrin had gathered men known for their ability to ignore the truth.

The high priest began to question Jesus concerning His teaching and His disciples. Reminding the priest of the popular response to what He taught, Jesus said:

"I have taught publicly. Ask those who've heard Me."

A brutal guard struck Him. Jesus asked:

"If I've said something wrong, say so. If I've spoken the truth, why hit Me?"

The witnesses contradicted one another, so the high priest dismissed them. To force the issue he demanded that Jesus answer the question he now posed:

"Are You the Messiah, the Son of God?"

Jesus declared:

"I am, and you will see the Son of Man coming in glory."

Annas was pleased. In his mind this was blatant blasphemy. He chose to ignore the wonders Jesus had worked, signs that testified to the truth of what He declared.

As priest Annas was ultimate judge of what was holy. The eyes of his soul refused to see the holiness of the One who now faced him. In the traditions of our people an unjust judge is among those most to be feared and condemned. Annas was one of those.

The old priest cried:

"He has blasphemed!"

To show his outrage, he tore his sacred robes. This was the ancient tradition. Hearing an unholy word, the priest, guardian of Israel's holiness, was to rip his holy robes.

Annas turned to the members of the Sanhedrin. He asked them:

"What is your judgment?"

The majority agreed:

"He's guilty and deserves to die."

Jesus was savagely beaten and spat upon. The guards covered His eyes and struck Him. As they rained their blows upon God's final revelation, His Word personified, they challenged Him:

"Messiah. Tell us who hit You!"

As light appeared in the eastern sky they led Jesus to the official high priest, Caiphas. The Sanhedrin followed. In the light of day they could lawfully meet as tribunal and reaffirm what they had done in the dark. Caiphas quickly approved their verdict.

We know now what they could not know then. It was the dawn of the day when the power of the dark was destroyed.

Jesus before Pilate

Pilate was annoyed. It was daybreak, the time he had told them to appear at his praetorium. They had not yet come, and he was waiting. He preferred to finish interviews and trials before midday.

He was even more annoyed when they arrived. They asked him to come out to them. Their reason being that the inner courtyard of the Roman governor was a Gentile place, and entering it would defile them.

As the Passover would begin in the evening, they claimed they'd have no time to purify themselves for the feast.

Roman officials were not accustomed to giving in to the demands of non-Romans. Fatefully, Pilate did that day. He slowly walked to the square outside this palace built by Herod the Great, the same Herod who'd tried to murder Jesus at His birth.

The mutual antipathy between Jew and Roman could be felt. The Roman looked out over the crowd from his platform and curled his lips. Making no attempt to conceal his scorn, he demanded:

"What charges do you bring against this Man?"

He knew well enough the charges, but he would force them to formally state their case. Replying in kind, they testily told him:

"If He were not a criminal, we would not have brought Him here."

Pilate gave Jesus a chance to answer His accusers, but He remained silent. His accusers perceived Pilate was not swayed by the very fact they had brought Jesus to trial. They feared the Roman might set Him free. To save their case, one of them called out:

"This Man claims to be a king."

This Pilate could not ignore. He could not let these hostile people see his hesitancy, so he had Jesus taken inside. There he asked Him:

"Are You the king of the Jews?"

"You are saying so," Jesus replied.

To clarify that He was no rival to Caesar nor to any earthly king, Jesus added:

"My kingdom does not belong to this world."

To stress the spiritual nature of His kingdom, Jesus added:

"Those who are seeking truth listen to Me."

Conscious of being Himself truth personified Jesus also implied that those seeking His death were not interested in truth. Pilate himself was not interested in what was for him a purely religious question. Jesus was beyond politics; Pilate was beyond religion's realm. He ended the discussion with a bored and skeptical:

"What is truth?"

Pilate saw that Jesus was innocent, and he searched for a way to exonerate Him. A solution seemed in sight; someone shouted that Jesus had always been a troublemaker, even in His native Galilee. Hearing He was a Galilean, Pilate sent a message to the ruler of Galilee, Herod Antipas, who was in Jerusalem for the feast.

Within a few minutes, Pilate's messenger had covered the short distance to the Hasmonean palace, where Herod was staying. Herod was curious and eager to see Jesus. Perhaps He would work a miracle. Let them bring Him. He would hear the case.

Brought before Herod, Jesus refused to speak. He knew Herod's heart. The man who had killed the Baptist was scarcely interested in just judgment. Jesus had nothing to say to him.

Disappointed, Herod quickly sent Jesus back to Pilate. In the meantime, Pilate had consulted a small group of close advisors. One of these became a Christian not long afterwards. He passed on to me what he recalled:

Pilate was a man much affected by dreams, and by his wife. Rising from bed and hearing of her husband's indecision, she sent a slave to him with a warning:

"Have nothing to do with that innocent Man. I had a terrible dream about Him this night."

This convinced Pilate. He had to extricate himself. As a Roman he knew the demands of justice. He also knew the sound he heard from the square outside, a crazed crowd demanding a death.

Filled with fear he walked outside. It was fear of a riot. His soldiers ringed the square, able and eager to show their skill. Still, even a suppressed riot would be reported to his immediate superior, Caesar's legate in Syria. The legate was no friend to Pilate.

Pilate's fear was matched by his hostility to the people he governed. He did everything he could to insult them, even as he gave way. This came out in his attempt to make Jesus benefit from his custom of releasing a prisoner on the feast of freedom. He asked if they would accept Jesus this year. They answered:

"Not this Man but Barabbas."

Jesus Barabbas was accused of murder in a riot. Seizing on the similarity of names, Pilate again offered to free Jesus of Nazareth. His way of identifying Jesus did not help to sway the mob:

"Why not accept Jesus called the Messiah?"

Furious, they insisted:

"Give us Barabbas."

Pilate gave them Barabbas. He gave Jesus into the hands of the soldiers, who further mistreated and mocked Him. These soldiers were not the usual garrison. They had been brought in to discourage trouble from a subject people celebrating their feast of freedom. Jesus represented for them the Jews they hated.

In hurting and degrading Jesus, these soldiers thought to hurt and degrade the Jewish race. They placed a bright red cloak over His shoulders and made a rude crown of thorns for His head. They then sank to their knees and saluted Him, as they would Caesar:

"Hail, king of the Jews!"

My source of information on this event was a young officer who was close to Pilate because of his noble birth. He was my age, and we became good friends. He told me:

"The sight of these armed men kneeling before Jesus came back to me in a dream. I dreamt that war and violence were submitting to peace."

This dream came to him later, after his conversion to Christ. He told me of this instant conversion:

"I entered the room where the soldiers were tormenting Jesus. I even joined in the abuse. I gave my own scarlet cloak to help complete the jest. As they placed my cloak on His shoulders I looked at Him. His eyes met mine, and I believed in Him."

The officer ordered the soldiers to cease their abuse and lead Jesus back to Pilate. At the sight of the bruised and bleeding Man he knew to be innocent, Pilate was moved. He was hopeful the sight would also move the crowd to pity. He had Jesus led out to them and proclaimed:

"Here is the Man."

Unmoved, the crowd shouted:

"Take Him away. Crucify Him."

I watched Pilate's look of incredulity change to spite as he asked:

"Shall I crucify your king?"

They shouted back:

"We have no king but Caesar. If you release this Man, you are no friend of Caesar."

Pilate knew Jesus was innocent, but he wanted to be Caesar's friend. He symbolically washed his hands in full view of the crowd and declared:

"I am not responsible for this Man's blood."

The mob shouted back:

"We are responsible."

Jesus was delivered to them. It was close to the noon hour.

The Way of the Cross

He was given the cross on which He would be nailed. It was only the crossbeam but so heavy He soon began to stumble. Jesus was a strong man, as I've said, and the distance He had to walk was not great. He was weakened, however, by a night of torture and privation of sleep and food.

To add to His suffering, the sand filled air and unseasonable heat had returned. The sky became darker as midday passed. It was as if nature had begun to mourn its Master. Women wept as Jesus staggered by. He managed to speak to them:

"Don't cry for Me, but for yourselves and for your children."

He was not rejecting their sympathy but referring to the sad fact that His suffering would not be appreciated by many of the people of Jerusalem. Two of these women, however, weighed His words. After His resurrection they came to believe and joined His disciples. I knew them well.

A man from Cyrene named Simon was on his way into the city. Just outside the gate, he stood aside to let them pass. His compassionate look was noticed by the soldiers. Wanting Jesus to reach the proper place of execution, they ordered the sturdy man to help Him carry His cross. Simon too was converted.

At last, Jesus arrived at Golgotha, called Calvary by the Romans. Considered a miscreant, He was crucified between two criminals. One of them reviled Him:

"Aren't You the Messiah? Why don't You save yourself and us?"

The other criminal repented. They were guilty of much more than stealing, but he is often called the Good Thief. He rebuked the reviler, reminding him they were both guilty. It was obvious that Jesus had done no wrong. With a sudden faith the Good Thief said:

"Jesus, remember me when You come into Your kingdom."

He heard the Lord answer:

"Today, you will be with me in paradise."

This "today" I now know to mean an eternal day, without time. As soon as Jesus says this word, it is beyond the limits of time. When He takes us into His own divine life, we too will step outside time, into the "today" that is always today.

We were all at a comparative distance, as close as the soldiers allowed. Although Jesus' voice was weak, I could hear this dialogue, and I could see the face of the Good Thief. He was not asking for an honor but simply to be with Jesus. It was a request Jesus never refused.

Pilate had ordered an inscription placed above Jesus' head:

"Jesus of Nazareth, King of the Jews."

Incensed, the chief priests demanded he change the title to read, "This Man said, I am King of the Jews."

By now, Pilate was in no mood for further concessions. With unwonted courage he sent them away, saying:

"What I have written, I have written."

Jesus' mother had come closer to the cross. Perhaps thinking of their own mothers, these coarse soldiers made way for her. She was simply dressed but had a dignity that set her apart. Mary was a little woman but a pillar of strength for us, that day and in the first days of our church.

Mary now stood by the cross on which her Son, the joy of her life, hung in agony. Her grief was too great for tears. Large nails held each of His arms and ankles to the wood. Blood was flowing from these great wounds and from His head and the ugly lacerations on His back and shoulders.

She longed to help Him down and hold Him in her arms. She had, instead, to watch His sacred head slowly sink towards His chest.

The soldiers said nothing as more of us came closer to the cross. Most of the women still stood at a distance, watching and waiting. Mary Magdalene came and stood on one side of Jesus' mother, John on the other.

Jesus could now barely see ahead, so low had His sacred head fallen, with nothing for support. He summoned enough strength to raise His head for a final gift. He spoke feebly but clearly:

"Woman, here is your son."

With a great effort He turned His head to John and said:

"Here is your mother."

Jesus would no longer be with Mary to care for her. Since He had no blood brothers but only cousins, whom we call "brothers," He gave His mother to His favorite cousin. John was the son of Salome, the sister of Mary, and much loved by her.

Even as His mother stood by, cruel onlookers continued to taunt Him. One of them called out:

"If You are the Son of God, if You can rebuild the Temple in three days, come down from the cross."

He was offered the customary drugged wine, to dull the pain. Dazed by His ordeal, Jesus tasted the wine but refused to drink more. His eyes were dimming. He could barely see the soldiers in front of Him casting dice for His clothing. Since His tunic had no seams, the soldiers cast dice to see which one would get it.

Reflecting on this scene in later years, we remembered the psalm of an innocent man persecuted by his enemies:

"They look at me and gloat. They divide my clothing among them and cast dice for my robe."

Meanwhile, Jesus prayed for His enemies:

"Father, forgive them. They do not know what they are doing."

During this time it had become dark, not the dark of night, but a dark that filled the day with gloom. We could see, but barely. Jesus spoke again, so faintly it was difficult to hear Him clearly. He murmured words that began with:

"Eli...."

This sounded to some as if He were calling for Elijah. They waited to see if Elijah would come to help Him. Our tradition linked that prophet to the Messiah. Elijah was to introduce his presence and assist him. Would he come now and help Him?

Mary told us she thought Jesus was pleading with His Abba, using the Syrian dialect of our ancient tongue, as He always did when outside the Temple or the synagogue. She thought she heard Him say:

"Eli, Eli, lama sabacthani?"

This is the opening cry of the first of the Psalms that form the core of our people's prayer. It is the cry of the faithful one in distress:

"My God, my God! Why have You left me alone?"

It is the final cry of the One who came among us, like us in everything but sin, enjoying friendships and food and drink and the beauties of nature, and also the suffering that is part of our lives. It was the cry of the human heart in agony so intense it feels abandoned, alone, and yet we too are never alone in our pain, as Jesus was not. Had He truly felt alone He would never have cried out to His Father. It is mystery, but His struggles were for us, and He is with us in our own struggles on this truly bumpy journey through life.

Our loveing Father is nearby,too, when we cry out.

This is what most of the disciples say they heard, that cry of terror and pain, but others are said to have heard Him say, "I am thirsty." Others thought they heard Him say, "Father into Your hands I entrust My spirit."

Another witness said he heard Jesus say, " it's finished." That is, I've done what I was born into this world to do....

The veil of the Temple was torn from top to bottom. This great veil had hidden the inner sanctuary from the rest of the Temple. This holy of holies had been God's special dwelling place among His people. His Son's death sundered the veil that had hidden and separated Him from His people.

Once a year, the high priest went beyond the veil into the inner sanctuary, carrying an offering of the blood of animals. Blood is a symbol of life, for without blood there is no life. The lives of animals had been offered as symbolic substitute for the lives of God's children. When He died for us Jesus entered the sanctuary of heaven with His own blood, as substitute for ours.

The Roman centurion in charge of the executions was converted on the spot. He said, with great conviction:

"This Man really was the Son of God!"

John took Mary to the home of her cousin, also named Mary, who had a house not far from Golgotha. At the same time those who had brought about Jesus' death hurried to Pilate to ask that the bones of the two criminals crucified with Him be broken. They would die quickly, and the bodies could be taken away before the Passover would begin, since our Law forbade that the bodies of criminals should hang on a gibbet on the Sabbath. Pilate gave permission. The soldiers broke the legs of the crucified criminals. They saw that Jesus had already died, but a soldier senselessly pierced His side with his lance. Blood and water flowed forth.

Meanwhile, evening was drawing near. The Sabbath would soon begin, at the setting of the sun. Joseph of Arimathea and Nicodemus, the two members of the Sanhedrin who were secret followers of Jesus, had gone to Pilate for leave to bury Jesus. Pilate granted this.

The two men hastily gathered aromatic spices and linens to prepare Jesus' body for burial. They had only a vague idea of what to do and found nobody to help. Temple servants were busy burying the two criminals and ignored them. The women were barred from helping them by the guard stationed there.

The women kept their watch. They noted the exact tomb and then left. They would return to anoint His body in a proper way as soon as they could. That would be the morning following the Sabbath.

Golgotha was just outside the city walls, bordering a rocky place used as a cemetery at that time by the well-to-do, especially. It was a garden, with the tombs scattered among the orange trees. Joseph had just completed hewing his own tomb from this nearby garden.

The two men laid a great linen cloth on the stone bed inside the tomb and spread aloes and myrrh on it. They tenderly took the body of their Lord down from the cross and placed it on the cloth, put more spices on the body and wrapped it. They rolled the stone across the entrance and left. A Temple guard was stationed at the spot, to see that no one stole the body.

. His body now lay lifeless in the tomb. A great Sabbath silence descended. I can now compare it to the great silence that had waited, before time began, for the word of God to give life where life had not been.

HE IS RISEN!

Very early in the mornng of the first day of the week, while it was still dark, a small group of women made their way towards the Tomb. They were the women who had kept watch while Jesus died and was buried. If I remember correctly, it was Mary Magdalene and Mary the mother of James the younger, Salome, the mother of James and John, and Joanna, wife of a high official in Herod's court.

They were hurrying, to get there before Peter and the others or the merely curious, or even Temple officials. They had procured aromatic oils to anoint Jesus' body more properly than the two men had been able to do. Salome raised a new problem:

"Who'll roll away the stone for us?"

They discussed this until they arrived. At that moment the first rays of the rising sun shone on the Tomb, dispersing the shadows and lighting the entrance. They stopped their chatter and stared. The stone had been rolled away. The Tomb was empty!

Mary Magdalene ran to tell Peter. She met him and John on their way to the Tomb. She gasped:

"They've taken the Lord away. We don't know where they've put Him."

Leaving Mary to catch her breath, Peter and John ran to the Tomb. John reached it first, but he waited for Peter to enter. Since Peter was now their leader, he should be the first to enter the Tomb.

Peter saw the linens laying on the floor. They cloth used to wrap Jesus' head was not with these linens but neatly folded and laying off by itself. It was obviously not the work of grave robbers. The other disciple felt in his heart that Jesus had risen, but he said nothing at the time.

Peter and his companion left, but the women stayed. Mary Magdalene soon rejoined them. The other women sat and rested against the orange trees. Mary sat alone, in front of the Tomb.

Later, the women said they felt as in a dream. Was it only delusion from fatigue and fasting, or had they really seen and heard angels? They thought they had. One or two, they were not sure. They agreed that the angel or angels announced Jesus had risen from the dead!

Here I have to admit that there are differing memories of exactly what happened, that is, the Eleven apostles said that Jesus first appeared to "Simon," that is, Peter. That is what I heard myself the evening of this wondrous day, but over the years another tradition has grown up, that it was to the Magdalene and the other women that Jesus first appeared. He probably first appeared to His mother, but as often Mary kept that in her heart; she shared her experiences with us only when she thought it important for our progressing in knowledge of her Son. Back to the scene at the Tomb that morning:

When the women told us the details we were hard put to piece them together. It was difficult to decide which woman had the more exact memory, for they disagreed! They all agreed on the one essential point, however: the Tomb was empty.

Jesus Appears at the Tomb

As Mary began to weep from strain and sorrow Jesus appeared. He asked her:

"Why are you weeping?"

She heard His voice. It was the same voice she had heard so often, but she was not expecting to hear it. Her whole attention was taken by her grief. She was looking at the empty Tomb and weeping over what had happened.

She thought it might be the gardener. He was caretaker of the garden and the tombs. Perhaps he had moved the Body? She said, without turning to look at the speaker:

"If you've moved His body, tell me where. I'll take care of it myself."

Jesus called her by name:

"Mary."

It was His voice! She turned and saw Him. At the same time, the other women saw Him and ran to Him. He told them not to cling to Him, as if to say He could not stay with them. They should go and tell the others He was risen from the dead.

On the Road to Emmaus

In the afternoon of that same day, two disciples were walking from Jerusalem to Emmaus. One of them was Cleophas, and I was the other. We wanted to get out of Jerusalem. I had property in the little place that was an easy two hours' walk. We could either return the same day or spend the night there, at Emmaus. Both of us favored the latter.

In those days there were more trees in this area. This was before the revolt of our people against the Romans, when most of the trees were cut down. On the road was an olive grove owned by a friend of my family. We stopped to quench our thirst at the well.

We drank and turned back towards the road. A man was standing there. He greeted us:

"Peace."

We returned his greeting with our "welcome."

He said he too was headed towards Emmaus, so we invited him to go along with us for the rest of our walk.

It was He, but we did not recognize Him. His physical appearance was not what it had been. His body was transformed. His voice was the same, but we did not associate it with Him.

He asked what we were discussing. In his blunt manner, Cleophas replied:

"You must be the only one in Jerusalem who hasn't heard what happened this weekend!"

"What happened?"

"Jesus of Nazareth, a prophet blessed by God and showing HIs power in word and deed, was handed over by our chief priests and elders to be condemned and crucified. We had hoped He would be the one to free Israel, but it's now the third day since this happened."

Just this morning some women of our little community told us things hard to believe. They were at His tomb before dawn and found it empty. They said they saw angels who declared He's alive. Others of our community went to the tomb and found it just as the women said, but they did not see Him"

The stranger spoke severely, with an authority that made us listen:

"How absurd. Why is it so hard for you to believe what the prophets foretold? They prophesied that the Messiah would have to suffer before entering into His glory."

As we walked along He recalled the passages in Scripture that clearly point to the Messiah as embodiment of Israel. Israel would suffer on her road to glory. Her suffering would be the result of her own sins and the sins of others. She was called a nation of priests, to offer expiation for other nations' sins.

The stranger cited several passages. One of the most notable is from the book of the prophet Isaiah:

"Who would have believed what we have heard?...no fine figure, no comeliness to charm us; disfigured, his beauty altered to something less than human...we despised him, something from which people avert their eyes. Yet, he bore our sufferings and endured our pain. We thought him struck by God...but he was pierced for our transgressions. By his scourging we are healed.

We had gone astray like sheep, but the Lord laid on him our guilt...he was taken away unjustly, cut off from the land of the living, though he had done nothing violent, spoken no deceitful word. Yet the Lord remembered His suffering servant and healed him who had made himself a sacrifice for sin...after his suffering he shall see the light."

We reached Emmaus. He said He would go on, but we pleaded with Him to stay. He had showed us the deeper meaning of the Scriptures we had heard so often. Although it was only mid-afternoon, we begged him:

"Stay with us, for evening is near. The day is almost over."

He did stay, and we sat down to break bread together. He took the loaf, blessed it and gave it to us. Then our eyes, the eyes of the soul, were opened! It was He! Then He disappeared.

Strange indeed. Even as He explained the Scriptures, our souls were seared. As He broke and blessed the bread, our souls were filled with light. We could recognize Him.

Why were we unable to recognize Him earlier? He was changed. The same body but transformed. As Mary Magdalene, so we too were not expecting to see Him. We too were so engrossed in our sadness and disappointment that we were unaware He was with us. No one else broke and blessed bread as He did.

"Peace"

Excited and overjoyed we returned to Jerusalem to share our experience with Peter and the others. We had to call in to them, for they had locked the doors. All day rumors had come concerning the hostile intentions of the Sanhedrin in their regard.

We recounted what had happened at Emmaus, and they said:

"It's true. He has risen and appeared to Peter!"

We were all talking at once. Suddenly, He was with us! The door was still locked, yet here He was. He greeted us:

"Peace."

This was no ordinary greeting. Even then we knew He was announcing His victory. When David or his successors as "anointed ones," that is, messiahs, returned from battle victorious, they were said to return in "peace."

Jesus was also announcing the end of alienation. Through His death and resurrection He had bridged the unbridgeable gap that had separated God from His people. He had won peace for the human race, harmony between God and His people, humankind.

He was wearing a white robe that hung loosely over His shoulders. Holding out His arms, He showed us the wounds in His hands and the gash in His side. The physical pain was gone, but the marks of the wounds endure. They remind us of the cost to Him of His love for us.

Jesus said again:

"Peace. As the Father has sent Me, I am sending you."

Then He breathed on us, as God had breathed His divine breath into the nostrils of Adam and Eve, to give life to the human race. Now He was giving new life, the life of the Spirit. a new era was at hand.

As He breathed His life giving spirit upon us, Jesus said:

"Receive the Holy Spirit. When you forgive sins, they are forgiven. When you do not, the are not forgiven."

You realize that this power to forgive or not to forgive must be in conformity with God's forgiving heart. Jesus intended His community to be a physical sign of the presence of the Spirit. In the end we are thrown upon God's mercy. The marks of Jesus' suffering for us should remind us of the extent of His merciful love.

Later that evening, within a few minutes, Thomas arrived; in our state of mind I had not noticed his absence. He was the prober, the stickler for exactness. He did not accept Peter's assurance that Jesus had appeared to them. He thought it was wishful thinking on their part:

"Unless I see the marks of the nails and put my hand on them and on the wound in His side, I'll not believe it."

This is what he said, but before you condemn him, remember: none of us had believed in Jesus' resurrection. We all had to see Him for ourselves. Thomas loved Jesus but wanted personal confirmation of his hope.

Jesus came again. This time Thomas was with us. Jesus invited him to touch His wounds and see that He had risen. Contrite, Thomas fell at His feet, and was inspired to declare:

"My Lord and my God!"

He spoke these words, but neither he nor we realized that God was revealing through him that Jesus is both Lord and God. Later we came to believe that Jesus is truly God as well as the man born of Mary. From this evening it was in our hearts but only with time did it dawn in our minds.

In things divine, love goes before reasoning. Many people saw Jesus and heard Him as He walked our holy land. Not everyone accepted His mission. This is only possible for those who love Him, who see Him with the eyes of the soul.

"Do You Love Me?"

Soon after this, the Eleven left for Galilee, where their families lived and where they could resume their work. All of them except Nathaniel were fishermen. The other disciples remained in Jerusalem, expecting them to return. They did, and they told of the times Jesus appeared to them.

The first time was at the sea of Galilee. Seven of them were there. At twilight Peter said he was going fishing. The other six said they'd go with him.

They stayed in the boat all the night long. In the uncertain light of early dawn they saw a man on the shore. It was common for fishermen to have a friend on the shore to direct them in the casting of the net. The man called to Peter:

"Have you caught anything?"

Peter yelled back:

"Not a single fish."

Although the light was unclear, the man seemed to see a school of fish. He directed Peter:

"Cast your net on the left side of the boat, and you'll find something."

Trusting the man's word, they did as He said. They caught so many fish they could hardly haul in the net, but the net was not broken. One of the disciples cried:

"It's the Lord!"

Peter jumped into the water and swam towards his Friend. The others followed, dragging their net behind the boat as they rowed ashore. Jesus had prepared a meal for them. Reflecting on this in the following months, especially after the gift of the Spirit at Pentecost, the disciples saw this meal as fulfillment of a promise Jesus had made to those who watch for Him in the night, to seat them at table and serve them. Of course, the ultimate fulfillment is the meal prepared for us in heaven.

John remembered something else of this event, Jesus asking them to count the fish. They counted one hundred and fifty three. We know that this was the number of the various types of fish, as was thought at the time. As fishers of people, Peter and the disciples should take in every type of person. We remembered the symbolism of the unbroken net, uniting all kinds of fish....

As they were finishing this most special meal Jesus gave Peter a chance to undo what he had done by denying his best Friend in His most difficult moment. At the last supper with His disciples Jesus had foretold that Peter would deny Him three times, that is, decisively. Now Peter was asked three times, decisively, to affirm his love for Jesus. He asked him:

"Do you love Me?"

Peter failed to see Jesus' intention. He was surprised and answered:

"You know I do."

Jesus asked him again, twice:

"Do you love Me?"

When Peter avowed he did indeed, Jesus appointed him shepherd of His flock. He told Peter::

"Feed My lambs, feed My sheep."

We see that Peter's authority was based on His love for Jesus and for His flock.

After this, Jesus appeared a final time to His disciples in Galilee. He assembled them for their mission. From the mountain He blessed them, saying:

"Go and make disciples of all peoples, baptizing them in name of the Father, and of the Son, and of the Holy Spirit. Teach them to carry out all I have commanded you."

His parting words: " I am with you till the end of time."

He was saying, to them and, to each of us: Don't be afraid. I'm close by, to guide you, to help you.

Still another way of putting it: You are not alone. I love you.

BIBLE TEXTS

Fr. James Kelly O.S.B. (1931-2006)

Born Clement Kelly, in Dansville, NY on August 20, 1931 to Clement and Caroline Kelly. Baptized in St. Patrick's Church, Dansville. Entered Mount Saviour Monastery on October 7, 1951. Clothed as postulant and receiving James as his name in religion on Nov. 1, 1951. Sent to St. Benoit-du-Lac in Canada, which at the time benevolently trained the novices of the recently (earlier in 1951) founded Mount Saviour, where he began his novitiate on July 22, 1952.

Pronounced his simple vows on July 25, 1953. Sent to study philosophy at Conception Abbey, MO. in September of that year and to S. Anselmo in Rome the following October to continue his studies for the priesthood. Ordained subdeacon at Assisi in 1956 and a deacon at the abbey of Subiaco in June of the following year (1957). Together with others from Mount Saviour studying at S. Anselmo he spent the summer of 1955 at the abbey of Maria Laach in the Rhineland, the summer of 1956 at the abbey of Engelberg in Switzerland, and the summer of 1957 at the abbey of Solesmes, France. On July 11, his solemn profession was received on behalf of Mount Saviour by Dom Ildefonso Rea, abbot of Monte Cassino in the newly restored basilica of that abbey.

Ordained to the priesthood by Bishop James Kearney at Mount Saviour on July 25, 1958. Returning to Rome to complete his studies just prior to the election of Bl. John XXIII, he received his S.T.L. from S.Anselmo in June, 1959. In December 1962 he was sent to aid the community of Dormition Abbey in Jerusalem, beginning studies at the Ecole Biblique in October of 1963, remaining in Jerusalem until June 1967. During these years he learned to converse in both Hebrew and Arabic and traveled on education trips to Egypt (several occasions, including visits to the then well nigh undiscovered Coptic monasteries), Iraq and Iran, several visits to Lebanon and Syria. On one of his visits to Turkey (1967) he was received and entertained by both the Orthodox Armenian patriarch Schnoik and by the Greek Orthodox patriarch Athenagoras, who introduced him to other Greek prelates as "Fr. James, my spiritual grandson." This same year, 1967, he received his S.S.L. from the Pontifical Biblical Commission.

Professor of Scripture at St. Bernard's Seminary, Rochester NY from 1968-1970, he began research as Visiting Fellow at Princeton Seminary in 1970 for his S.T.D. with specialization in Scripture received from the Antonianum in Rome, after further studies at the Franciscan Biblical Institute in Jerusalem. He was Visiting Scholar at Cambridge University in 1977-78 and served as campus minister to Hobart College 1979-81 and to Cornell University 1981-83, as well as at St. Leo College 1983-86. He subsequently served as civilian chaplain to the U.S. Army in Germany,1987-90 (Nuremberg) and to the U.S. Dept. of Defense at Bad Aibling, near Munich, from 1990-1994. Since then he has remained at Mount Saviour, occasionally giving Scripture workshops both at Mount Saviour and in parish communities, in addition to serving as Mount Saviour's outreach to the poor in the form of preaching once per month on behalf of Food for the Poor.

He finished the book a few days before he died in his sleep before the Easter Vigil on April 16th, 2006.

Printed in the United States
64230LVS00002B/1-99